Genesis - Deuteronomy

Through the Bible with

Lance Lambert

Genesis - Deuteronomy

Through the Bible with

Lance Lambert

LANCE LAMBERT MINISTRIES

Richmond, Virginia, USA

Illustration on p. 91 by Anna Yao

ISBN: 978-1-68389-045-4

www.lancelambert.org

Contents

Introduction

As part of the *Through the Bible* series, this volume begins the study at the very beginning: the genesis of the Word of God. These volumes were compiled from a series Lance shared with the brothers and sisters at Halford House in Richmond, Surrey. Lance himself went back through this series later in life and provided a study guide to accompany these lessons. We have included this guide to these volumes as a help to enhance your studies.

Other volumes are yet to come, but currently you can find two volumes by Lance on *How the Bible Came to Be*. The second of these volumes has two extra chapters on how to study the Bible that are beneficial guides to get us started in digging into the Word for ourselves. What a blessing it is to have the living Word of God! May we search out God's treasures within it.

Please note that these volumes are derived from actual Bible studies and have been kept very close to the original with very minor edits.

1.
Genesis:
A General Survey

Reading the Word in Preparation for Study

Whilst it may be interesting and instructive to talk *about* the Bible, after all, we have only one end in view, and that is to study the Word itself. I would like to say, now that we have reached this point, how very necessary it is that you should, without any coercion or persuasion from me, be reading in the week preceding, as much as you can of what we are going to study on Friday[1]. Otherwise, as I once did, you are only going to find the same as I have found. I used to always say to myself: "Now, I must read, I must read that chapter or that letter through." Then the night came, and, of course, whilst I gained quite a lot from that time, I was very sorry at the time that I had not read it. Then I always used to say to myself, "I will read it. I shall read it this coming week and

---

1. Please note the text comes from Bible studies held at Halford House and has been edited only minimally for clarity and grammatical purposes.

get down to it," but never did. So, it is by far the best thing to be quite strong and definite with ourselves in the week preceding, and say, "Now, I am going to put aside a certain amount of time this week to really read, even if I do not understand it, just to read it, to get the background," so that when we come to this time on Friday, we know something of the context.

Now, you should have read the first three chapters of Genesis. We cannot, this evening, now read them together. We will read the first chapter of Genesis because all the time I am going to be making references to these three chapters. You really do need to know something of what is in them. I wonder if we could read together this first chapter:

> *In the beginning, God created the heavens and the earth. And the earth was waste and void; and darkness was upon the face of the deep: and the Spirit of God moved upon the face of the waters. And God said, Let there be light: and there was light. And God saw the light that it was good: and God divided the light from the darkness. And God called the light Day, and the darkness he called Night. And there was evening and there was morning, one day.*

> *And God said, Let there be a firmament in the midst of the waters, and let it divide the waters from the waters. And God made the firmament, and divided the waters which were under the firmament from the waters which were above the firmament: and it was so. And God called the firmament Heaven. And there was evening and there was morning, a second day.*

And God said, Let the waters under the heavens be gathered together unto one place, and let the dry land appear: and it was so. And God called the dry land Earth; and the gathering together of the waters called he Seas: and God saw that it was good. And God said, Let the earth put forth grass, herbs yielding seed, and fruit-trees bearing fruit after their kind, wherein is the seed thereof, upon the earth: and it was so. And the earth brought forth grass, herbs yielding seed after their kind, and trees bearing fruit, wherein is the seed thereof, after their kind: and God saw that it was good. And there was evening and there was morning, a third day.

And God said, Let there be lights in the firmament of heaven to divide the day from the night; and let them be for signs, and for seasons, and for days and years: and let them be for lights in the firmament of heaven to give light upon the earth: and it was so. And God made the two great lights; the greater light to rule the day, and the lesser light to rule the night: he made the stars also.

And God set them in the firmament of heaven to give light upon the earth, and to rule over the day and over the night, and to divide the light from the darkness: and God saw that it was good. And there was evening and there was morning, a fourth day.

And God said, Let the waters swarm with swarms of living creatures, and let birds fly above the earth in the open firmament of heaven. And God created the great sea-

monsters, and every living creature that moveth, wherewith
the waters swarmed, after their kind, and every winged
bird after its kind: and God saw that it was good. And God
blessed them, saying, Be fruitful, and multiply, and fill the
waters in the seas, and let birds multiply on the earth. And
there was evening and there was morning, a fifth day.

And God said, Let the earth bring forth living creatures after
their kind, cattle, and creeping things, and beasts of the earth
after their kind: and it was so. And God made the beasts of
the earth after their kind, and the cattle after their kind, and
everything that creepeth upon the ground after its kind: and
God saw that it was good. And God said, Let us make man
in our image, after our likeness: and let them have dominion
over the fish of the sea, and over the birds of the heavens, and
over the cattle, and over all the earth, and over every creeping
thing that creepeth upon the earth. And God created man
in his own image, in the image of God created he him; male
and female created he them. And God blessed them: and God
said unto them, Be fruitful, and multiply, and replenish the
earth, and subdue it; and have dominion over the fish of the
sea, and over the birds of the heavens, and over every living
thing that moveth upon the earth. And God said, Behold, I
have given you every herb yielding seed, which is upon the face
of all the earth, and every tree, in which is the fruit of a tree
yielding seed; to you it shall be for food: and to every beast of
the earth, and to every bird of the heavens, and to everything
that creepeth upon the earth, wherein there is life, I have
given every green herb for food: and it was so. And God saw

everything that he had made, and, behold, it was very good.
And there was evening and there was morning, the sixth day.

And then we will just read the first four verses of chapter 2 because there should not be a chapter division there. Actually, chapter one really ends with verse 4 of chapter 2:

And the heavens and the earth were finished, and all the host of them. And on the seventh day God finished his work which he had made; and he rested on the seventh day from all his work which he had made. And God blessed the seventh day, and hallowed it; because that in it he rested from all his work which God had created and made. These are the generations of the heavens and the earth when they were created, in the day that Jehovah God made earth and heaven.

The Importance of the First Three Chapters of Genesis

There are two or three things I want to say generally. We are taking the first three chapters of the Bible because they are absolutely essential and elementary to every single thing within the Bible. That is what most people fail to realise: there is not one major doctrine which does not, in some way, evolve from these three chapters, and it is probably the answer to the controversy which has raged over them. It is these three chapters that are always called myths and fables which cannot be relied upon. Modern science has shown that it is hopelessly incorrect and inaccurate and so on. However, the point really is, that within these three chapters we have everything. If we had no Bible, we have really everything within these three chapters. Of course, what we have often said is that the Bible is progressive in its revelation. That is, as you go on, it reveals more and more and more. But everything is found in seed form in these three chapters. You will find the church, the gospel, the cross, the Lamb slain, and God's eternal purpose all within these three chapters. You will find everything within these three first chapters of the Word of God.

The Uniqueness of the First Three Chapters of Genesis

The first thing I want you to note about these chapters is that their ancient character in literary method, style, and vocabulary is quite unique. When you are dealing with the first three chapters, in fact, actually the first almost twelve chapters of Genesis, you are dealing with one of the oldest documents in world history. And as we would expect, the vocabulary, the style, and the method, are all absolutely within keeping to their age. You will remember that many people a hundred years ago thought that writing was not even known in the days of Moses. They now believe that writing was known thousands of years earlier than Moses. It is quite feasible, indeed I think it is more than feasible, it is probable that the first chapter of Genesis up to chapter 2 verse 4 is the earliest written document in history. Certainly everything about it is ancient. As you read through the first three chapters of Genesis you will not find one really hard word. They are all, generally speaking, one or two syllable words. Quite simple. Its simplicity is quite remarkable.

Another thing that is also very interesting is the style. It is terse. In the Hebrew it is even more terse than in English. Things such as verse 3: "God said, 'Let there be light,' and there was light." In Hebrew it is just "Let light be and light was." It is as simple and terse as that. That is the style of these three chapters. If you read right through them you will find them terse and simple and direct.

Another remarkable thing about these chapters is their literary method. One of the most ancient Hebrew methods was what is called parallelism. That is, it was a form of poetry. There was a little introduction, followed by three thoughts and then, parallel with them, another three thoughts. Here you have that method. First of all, in the first two verses there is an introduction. Then you have three days—one, two, three. Parallel with them, you have another three days, and then you have the conclusion.

After that, you have what is called the *colophon* in ancient literature. Particularly with tablets, they had a colophon, which just said at the end who was the writer or author. And here we have it in verse 4: "These are the generations ..." That word *generations* is the word *toledoth* in Hebrew, which means "history" or "book." And indeed, in the Septuagint version it is translated: "This is the book of the history of the creation of the heavens and the earth." And the author is the Lord God. Evidently, the revelation was committed to man by the Lord, Himself. Jewish tradition tells us that this revelation was given to Enoch and that he was the first man, according to the Jewish rabbis, ever to write. And he committed it to writing.

Now, when we take the whole book of Genesis, we shall be going into this question of tablets, clay tablets, and early forms of writing and so on, particularly in the book of Genesis. I just wanted to mention that to you. That is the first thing.

The Timelessness of the First Three Chapters of Genesis

There is a second thing I want to mention to you. Have you ever realised the timelessness of these three chapters? One of the common and rather stupid remarks that we often hear made is: "Oh, it is so unscientific! Science contradicts these things. I cannot believe the beginning of the Bible. It is not scientific." But just supposing that the first three chapters of Genesis had been put into scientific terminology–no one, all through the history of man would have been able to understand it until the twentieth century. And one of the most remarkable things about these three chapters is the way they have been set forth in a way that every generation from the beginning have been able to understand. The very ancient peoples always spoke in a symbolical and in a very, very simple and direct way. I have been fortunate and blessed in one way to study classical Chinese. And in classical Chinese, everything is terse and simple. The earlier you go, the older the manuscripts, the more simple, and the more direct they are. It might all seem very mythical, but it is all put in very, very simple form.

These three chapters of Genesis have survived the whole history of humanity and in every generation have been understood even by the gardener. Isn't that wonderful? And yet if they had been put in scientific terminology, it would have sealed this book up entirely. No one would have understood it until the twentieth century and then only by certain scientific minds who are versed in all the scientific terminology and the ideas there. That is something I find very, very interesting and very, very wonderful.

The Creation Story

Another thing I want to point out is that the creation story is preserved either in a fragmentary form, or in a very much more embossed form, in nearly every race and nation in the world. That is one of the most remarkable things. The Chinese of course have this story, as well as the story of the flood. It is much more embellished and embossed than the Biblical account. Much more has come into it, with gods and goddesses all over the place. In Chinese mythology, the story of the flood has eight people being saved. They went to a boat and were saved in a flood. Inca tradition also has the story of creation, very much the same as this. It also has the story of the flood. And we could mention many, many other nations that have this story in their history, as well. The interesting thing is that the only clear and full account, indeed the most practical account is the account that we have in the Bible. All the other great accounts—the Babylonian, the Chinese, the Incan, and many other great civilisations—have within them a lot that you just cannot swallow. It is quite obviously mythological. I just say that also in passing.

Two Accounts Of Creation

One of the great controversies that has centred upon Genesis has been the supposed two contradictory accounts of creation.

And if you have read the first three chapters, you will have seen it quite clearly. The first account in Genesis 1, seems to contradict the account in Genesis 2. In Genesis 1 everything is created and ends with God creating man and woman. Then we have a duplication in Genesis 2, which seems as if the whole story is retold from a completely different source. And the Modernists will tell us that different words are used and different titles are used for God, and the whole context is different. Man is made first and then all the other things: the beasts, the flowers, the plants and everything else come after him. And when all that has happened, woman is created. It is entirely a contradiction to Genesis 1. There are two entirely different accounts. And they say that Moses was a somewhat ignorant man and he, to put it crudely, hashed up his work of editing. Instead of ruling out everything and making two accounts into one thoroughly good account, he very superficially glossed over them and left these two accounts there. And even more amusing, Genesis 3:1–8, is the same as chapter 1. So this account somehow got pushed in again after chapter 2. So, those are some of the ideas that have surrounded these chapters.

As we look at these three chapters, what is the key? Why has the Holy Spirit duplicated the account of creation in chapter 2? And what is the key to this obvious use of different words? Why does chapter 1 use certain words and chapter 2 use other words? What is the key to it? Well, if you get this clearly in your mind, I think it will help you greatly.

Genesis 1 is the fact of creation—from whence, and how. From where did it all come? How did it come? From where did this universe come? From where did man and woman come? From where did life come? From where did this whole design and harmony come? And how did it come into being? What was the method? Can you give me a clue to the method? Genesis 1 is the clue to where it came from and how it came into being. It is the fact of creation.

Genesis 2 has an entirely different object and that is why the whole thing is turned round in a different way with a meaning. Genesis 1 is the actual process of creation, the order, if you like. Genesis 2 is the purpose of creation, or unto what and why. Where is it all going? And why is it all here? What is the goal? And if that is the goal, why? That is Genesis 2.

Genesis 3 is the fall of creation, the explanation of the present and the answer. It is very wonderful. The answer is in Genesis 3. The answer is there, the explanation of the present. In other words, supposing you are in a kindergarten and you are asking questions. You say to your teacher, "Where does this world come from?" Then he answers you. Then you ask another question: "But how?" You are answered. "Well, what is the purpose of it? What is the aim?" You are answered. "But why?" And you are answered. Then you may well turn around and say, "But that doesn't tie up with what we have at present. What has happened since?" And Genesis 3 is the explanation of the present. What has happened and God's answer to what has happened. Is that clear?

The Names of God in Genesis 1–3

Elohim

The next thing I want you to note is the titles or names that are used for God in these three chapters because in their use is, again, a key. In Genesis 1, the name Elohim is used absolutely exclusively. We should get an understanding of this name because it appears all the way through Scripture. "In the beginning God ..." And right the way through Genesis 1 this is used exclusively for God—Elohim. Its root meaning is "the Mighty or the Strong One," and it always brings into view the God of creation. Whenever Elohim is used it is always bringing into view God as the God of all creation. You get its form used in many other names such as El Elyon, "the Most High;" Daniel uses that always. Or El Shaddai, "God the Almighty." Then, you get it in El Bethel, "God, of the House of God." So we find it all the way through Scripture—El, God, Elohim in full, God. We will come to that again in a moment because it is very, very wonderful.

We find Elohim used again and again and again in Genesis 1: "God said ... God called ... God divided ..." God did this. God did that. God, the God of all creation. It brings into view the majesty, the grandeur, and the immensity of God. Now, mark that because in the 20th century that is what is lacking—the majesty, the grandeur, and the immensity of God.

Even among Evangelicals, this is the thing that is sadly lacking. Our God is so small. There is no longer that sense of the greatness of God, the sovereignty of God, the almightiness of God. It is a tremendous thing. The whole spirit of the 20th century is to belittle God and make Him into some little departmental being that is not really sovereign and cannot really do anything He wants to do. But Elohim speaks of the mightiness and the immensity of God.

Jehovah

In Genesis 2, the name Jehovah is used exclusively. Jehovah God, the two are brought together. Yahweh Elohim, the Lord God, Jehovah God or Jehovah Elohim. We do not even really know how that name is pronounced because the Jews were never ever allowed to utter it. You always had to be silent, pass it over, or substitute another word for it. So we do not even know how it was pronounced. But we think it was pronounced Yahweh. Jehovah. This name, wherever you find it in Scripture, speaks of the intimate God of redeeming love; the name by which He wanted to be known in the most inner, intimate, marriage bond between Himself and His people. He did not want them just to know Him as Elohim. He wanted His own to know Him as Jehovah. And there is something so very, very wonderful about the name Jehovah. You can think of it as the Covenant God, the Covenant Keeping God, the God who has bound Himself to His people by love, by His own faithfulness. He has come down to their level and bound Himself to them. The great God of creation has come right down to intimate, personal, direct level and bound Himself to each of us as His people. And He says, "I will love thee with an everlasting love." Do you see? That is Jehovah, and it brings into view the grace and the love and the mercy and the faithfulness of God.

Now, whenever you read Jehovah in your Bible, think about that. It means that when the Lord says, "I am Jehovah," He is always trying to make them think, you see? When He speaks to them as El Shaddai, He is trying to tell them something else. But when He speaks to them as Jehovah, He is trying to awaken cords of love in His people. He is saying, "I am the faithful One.

I am the One who is full of love for you, and mercy toward you, and grace for you.

The wonderful thing is, and this might surprise you, that the root meaning of Jehovah is "to be." " I AM." Do you remember what He said to Moses? "I AM that I AM. Go and say that I AM has sent you." I AM has come down to us as Yahweh, as Jehovah. What does it mean? God wants to link His eternity, His unchangeableness, to the fact of His faithfulness. That is very wonderful! In other words, He is not faithful for an age, He is not faithful for ages. He is faithful for eternity. The root form, the root meaning of Jehovah is "unchangeableness," and He has linked that with grace, and love, and mercy, and faithfulness. We would have thought that the unchangeableness would have been linked with the God of creation, wouldn't we? But no, that is where we are wrong. Creation is more transient than the mercy and the love of God. The love of God, in God's sight, is the eternal thing; this creation is the transient thing.

Genesis 1 uses Elohim; Genesis 2 uses Jehovah Elohim, combining the God of creation with the God of redeeming love. That is very wonderful, isn't it? And then, something that you might want to note, in Genesis 3, when the devil comes to Eve, he never mentions God by the name Jehovah. Isn't that interesting? Of course, the dear old Modernists, have got all their own theories for this. They have decided that there are the "E" documents and the "J" documents and the "P" documents and all this kind of business. They try to get around what the Holy Spirit is saying by saying that these were written by all different kinds of people, that these are fragments brought together in a very poor way. However, Genesis 3 begins like this: "Now the serpent was more subtle than any beast of the field which the Lord God, (or Jehovah God) had made. And he said unto them, 'Yea, hath God said?'"

All the way through, the serpent speaks of Him just as God. The God of creation, Elohim. And do you know the tragedy? When Eve replies she says, "For God doth know ..." That was the beginning of the fall. It was the name; it is rather interesting in that way. The devil was going to keep off the redeeming side of God's nature with a very real purpose in view. I hope you realise that. He hoped that when the woman had fallen, she would be so terrified that she would never recover from it. But the wonder of it is that God made Himself known to them as the redeeming God of love. Even though He had to put them out of the Garden, He made Himself known to them as the redeeming God. So, in Genesis 1 we have Elohim; in Genesis 2 we have Jehovah.

The Words *Bara*, *Asah*, and *Yatsar*

Now, I want you to note the words "create," "make," and "form." The first one is the Hebrew word *bara* and is used three times in Genesis 1. The first time is in verse 1: "In the beginning God created the heavens and the earth." Verse 21: "And God created the great sea monsters, and every living creature that moveth, wherewith the waters swarmed, after their kind, and every winged bird after its kind ..." Verse 27: "And God created man in His own image, in the image of God created He him; male and female created He them."

It is not quite known from where the word *bara*, "to create" came originally. Possibly, it came from a root word which meant "to cut off; to cut off a piece, and then to work on it". But in this context, it always means a definite, sovereign act of creation. In other words, whenever the word *bara* is used, it means that God is doing a new thing. It has no relationship to what we see, and that is very important.

This word is used three times. God created the heavens and the earth without anything pre-existing. He created. It was an act of sovereign creation. God created the sea monsters and the things that swarm in the water and the birds, the winged creatures. That is the beginning of animate life. The word is used again, creation. God created. And then, when it comes to man, human life, God created; it was a sovereign act of creation. It was absolutely sovereign. In other words, it was by the Word of God and it was sovereign. That is the method; it was sovereign. This word is used elsewhere in the Word, but in these three chapters, it is only used in Genesis 1, and these are the three times.

The second word that is used, and it is used approximately 2,500 times in the Old Testament, is the word *asah*, and it means nearly everything, quite honestly. To know exactly what it does mean, you have to rely on context like you do with many ancient languages. But here it means "to make, to do, or to fashion." And this word, *asah*, always means you are fashioning something which already exists. That is very important. In other words, you are working on something which is already there.

Creation, the word "create," or *bara*, means either you bring something out of nothing, or you are doing something with the material without any relationship to what it was before. In other words, no evolution; it is a sovereign act. *Asah* is quite different. It is taking something like clay, or something like that, and moulding it, fashioning it. There may be a process in it.

It is very, very wonderful. This word is used in verses 7, 16, 25, and 31 of Genesis 1.

And then, this is the wonderful thing, Genesis 2 has a different word. It is the word *yatsar* and this word means "to form or to fashion. " It is generally used of the potter and the clay—to form or to fashion. *Yatsar* is used in Genesis 2:7, 8, and 19. "The Lord God formed man out of the dust of the ground."

This word *yatsar* is really very, very thrilling to investigate. It means, in some connections, not here, but in some connections, to "pre-ordain or to devise or to plan." Today, as you know, Arabic is the only modern language that in any way corresponds to ancient Hebrew. And in Arabic today, the word *yatsar* is still used for covenant or contract, and that is very very, wonderful.

Now let's bring it all together. In Genesis 1 you have Elohim—the God of all creation—His immensity, His grandeur, His majesty. And that word used in Genesis 1 is *bara*. God creates out of nothing; it is sovereign activity. Then the word *asah* is also used. The God of creation is fashioning and moulding. It is method that is the point there. But in Genesis 2, when you have Jehovah in view, it is the potter and the clay. He is planning something. He is purposing something. He is, as it were, contracting something. He has something in mind, and He is working it to the end. He is fashioning something. It is very, very wonderful how the Holy Spirit has chosen the words of these three chapters. We have those two accounts of creation, and they have been carefully worded.

Thus, in the fact of creation, you have got Elohim, acting quite sovereignly. Even when the word *asah* is used, it still relates to God's sovereign activity—the birds and the fish and the sea monsters, which we may look at a little more closely—may well have evolved. There may be a process in their creation which is within the word, the word suggests it, implies it. However, behind the process is creation, the word *bara* is used of it. In other words, it is still God. Whatever the method that is used in Genesis 1 for creation in this universe, it is the God of sovereign activity that is behind it. Whether He is bringing something into being that was never there before, as the heavens and the earth, or whether He is bringing out of the waters, causing the waters to swarm with swarming things, (the word literally means "teem with teeming things") or whether He is causing the winged things, which are insects and birds of every kind, to come into being, maybe out of the water, (it is a possibility that it had something to do with the water to begin with) or whether it is the sea monsters, or whether He is doing a new thing altogether, as with man, He is the God of sovereign activity. He is doing a new thing, quite differently. He takes the clay of the ground and moulds it and then breathes into it and man becomes a living soul.

Elohim: A Plural Noun

There is another thing I want you to know. This word, Elohim, is very, very interesting. It is a word which is plural. Now, isn't that wonderful? It is a thing the rabbis could never get over; they could never understand it. The rabbis always got over it by saying "Well, it must mean that God had fellowship with the angels." Because Elohim is in the plural and really is a plural noun, it is, as it were, gods and yet not gods. The idea is a plurality in unity. Well, isn't that the Trinity? And we find it in the first three or four words of the Bible: "In the beginning God ..." Now, here is another wonderful thing. This noun Elohim is always used with a verb in the singular. The thought is that the Trinity is moving in unity all the time. "In the beginning God created ..." as One Person. The rabbis could never understand this. Of course, when they came down to Genesis 2, the whole Trinity is there.

Chapter 1:1 says "In the beginning God [Elohim] created ..." The word for God here is, as I have already said, in the plural; and "created" is in the singular. Verse 2 says, "The Spirit of God moved upon the face of the waters." The Spirit of God moved, or hovered upon the face of the waters. We find the third person of the Trinity mentioned there. Now look at verse 26: "God said, 'Let us make man in our image and after our likeness. And let them have dominion.'" That is very remarkable, isn't it? "Let us ..." speaking of God. And then in chapter 3:22, "The Lord God said, 'Behold the man has become as one of us, to know good and evil.'" The rabbis could never understand that and they always said it was God talking with the angels and saying, "Let us make ..." But surely that is not quite right. The angels did not actually join a sovereign equality with God in the creation of this world, did they? They are themselves a creation. So here is the first and earliest inference to the Trinity—God the Father, God the Son, and God the Holy Spirit. They are working here together.

The name Jehovah is a name that is peculiarly associated with the Lord Jesus. And the tree of life of course is again, something that is associated with the Lord Jesus. He said, "I am the Life. I am the True Vine". A lot that is associated with this tree of life relates to the garden. So we have there the whole Trinity in covenant together in the creation of the universe and the creation of man. We have it all.

God's Eternal Purpose

Thus, in these first three chapters of Genesis, we have God the Father, God the Son, and God the Holy Spirit. We also have the eternal purpose of God. Now, where do we find the eternal purpose of God in these three chapters? First of all, we see it in the tree of life in the midst of the garden. The tree of life is associated with the eternal purpose of God. Do you know what it means? It means a humanity in utter dependence for its life and the fulfilment of its responsibility on Christ. That is, God's purpose was that humanity could only live, (really Live, with a capital "L," not this living death), insofar as humanity is utterly dependent on Christ. And it could only fulfil its responsibility to have dominion over all things insofar as it was dependent on Christ. That is the eternal purpose of God and it is summed up in the man and the woman, the institution of marriage. Many people think that marriage is something that was instituted for our benefit. Of course, it was instituted for the reproduction of humanity, but primarily it was to show forth, in picture form, the eternal purpose of God. Marriage is the symbol of the eternal purpose of God because the end is humanity in union with God, in utter union with God, and in utter dependence on God. The woman was taken out of man's side and fashioned. In other words, she was not formed as man; she was taken out of man in the same way that humanity is, as it were, taken out of Christ. That is the thought. By eating the tree of life she would become incorporated into Christ, in union with Christ, in such a union of dependence and mutual fellowship and love, that the whole question of responsibility for the universe was to be fulfilled.

You may sum up the eternal purpose of God in two things: Christ the centre and sum of all and, secondly, a people in union with Christ. That is the eternal purpose of God. Christ the sum and the centre, the centre and sum of all, and then a people in union with Christ.

The Probation and the Fall

In these first three chapters, you have the probation of man and the fall. That is, something awful happened and the whole thing was wrecked from the beginning, but mind you, wrecked in such a way that even when we come to know the Lord, our greatest battle is with our own deceived selves. Something happened at that fall which has left an amazing mark. So intricate and so deep is the work of Satan in humanity, it can be seen in every way. It can be seen in the absolutely spontaneous distrust of God. And that is one of our biggest battles when we come to the Lord, a quite spontaneous distrust of the Lord. It can be seen in the way that humanity was blinded utterly to God's character, quite blinded to what God is like. And then it can be seen in every single way in man. The whole relationship between a husband and wife has been smashed beyond recognition, so that, by the very curse itself, the whole thing became perverted and reoriented. It became a thing that binds people, chains people, and fetters people all their lives.

Corruption came in there. Man became a slave to the thing over which he should have had dominion. By the sweat of his brow he had to earn his living. And the ground, instead of being flexible and pliable, yielded thorns and thistles and briers. Everything got on top of him, so that man is now under it all, absolutely under it. That is all in the first three chapters of Genesis, and oh, if people would only read them, what an understanding they would come to of themselves and of what Satan has done in us. But thank God, there is not only the probation and the fall in those first three chapters, there is also the cross and the Lamb slain. Those are all in the first three chapters of Genesis.

God Rebukes Satan

When the fall came, you would have thought that God would have turned round and blamed man, blamed woman. But, no, the first words God had of rebuke were for Satan. And God said these wonderful words, "I will put enmity between thee and the woman, and between thy seed and her seed. He shall bruise thy head and thou shall bruise His heel." Of course this is a very, very old reference. But Eve knew what He was talking about. And it is a very wonderful thing that a bit later Adam called Ishsha, "taken out of me," he called her Eve, "the mother of all living." That is very, very wonderful, because Adam had come into the realm of death, but he called Eve the mother of all living. Do you know why? It is because she said, "I have gotten a man with the help of the Lord." She really wondered, I think, at the very beginning, as to whether her first born was going to be the deliverer, there and then, as we all do. We like to believe it is going to be right within our lifetime. Eve really wondered whether this was the Messiah, straightway.

The Lord's Promise

What was the Lord's promise? He said the most amazing thing. He said that humanity, from henceforth, was to be divided into two streams, the seed of the serpent and the seed of the woman. What an awful thing that is, the seed of the serpent and the seed of the woman. The seed of the woman is what we call the good seed, or the godly seed. The seed of the serpent is what we call the evil seed or the bad seed. It began right there. Cain was of his father the devil. He was of the bad seed. Abel was of the good seed and so was Seth who replaced him. You remember Cain slew Abel.

Here we have got two great streams of humanity. One line comes from Enoch, Noah, Terah, Abraham, Isaac, Jacob, Joseph, Moses, and so on, right the way down to the Messiah. On the other line you have got the evil seed; it is a terrible story. Cities come into being as a product of the evil seed. Cities were a product of the evil seed, and music, and murder, fornication and adultery. Every kind of evil came in as the seed of the serpent. We are all born, naturally, as the seed of the serpent, which is the most terrible thing. But we can all become the seed of the woman. Isn't it a wonderful thing, as someone has said, that there, at the very beginning, was the virgin birth? Not the seed of man, but the seed of the woman, the seed of the Holy Ghost.

The Cross and the Lamb

I have just one other thing to say, and it is all in these three chapters—the cross and the Lamb. Where is the cross? "I will put enmity between thy seed and her seed." And that is the story of humanity: the violent hatred of the bad seed for the good seed, such a hatred as would blot out the good seed whenever it is possible and destroy it; and that has always been the way. But listen to this: "He shall bruise thy head and thou shall bruise his heel." What does that mean? It means that the cross, as it were, was the smashing of Satan's head and all Satan could do was to bruise the heel of the Messiah. In other words, the death of the Lord Jesus is looked upon as the bruising of His heel because He rose again. However, the cross is looked upon as the slaying of Satan, the decapitating of Satan. His head was smashed and all he could do was bruise the heel of the Messiah. That is the cross, and it is promised there in Genesis 3.

God's Covering for Man

And then, of course, the most wonderful of all is verse 21: "The Lord God made for Adam and for his wife coats of skin and clothed them." This is very, very wonderful. The wonderful fact is that, in Genesis 3, we have the beginnings of something which has become woven into our old nature. Isn't it a strange thing that as soon as Adam and Eve fell, they became self-conscious? It is rather unpleasant to talk about, but that was one of the great marks of the fall. (Actually, there is a good deal more that happened by the fall, more than self-consciousness, which I leave you to find out there in the Word.) They went further than that. They went and stitched themselves aprons of leaves. Well, we may think that is very commendable. Having suddenly discovered that they were naked, and become extremely self-conscious, they stitched themselves aprons of leaves. And why didn't the Lord sort of say, "That is most commendable of you. You have covered your sins"? But the fact is that now they were empty and aimless and miserable. They had lost the glory. They had lost their original state and condition. But do you know what the Lord did? He took them and He made them clothes of skin.

Some people, rather foolishly, say how unjust and severe God was with Cain because he brought the fruits of the ground, whereas Abel brought a little lamb, the firstling of the flocks. Abel was accepted and Cain was rejected, so people say it seems a bit unfair. But the whole point was this: there could have been nothing more vivid in the mind of Adam and Eve, than this. When they had made themselves clothes of leaves, God, as it were, undressed them again, and gave them clothes of skin. This means that no natural, self-made covering can possibly give us access before God. The only thing that can cover us is the death of another. With leaves there was no death, but with skins, there was the death of a lamb and the blood of a lamb. "... apart from shedding of blood there is no forgiveness" (Hebrews 9:22b). So their sin was forgiven and covered. And although God put them out of the garden, He did so out of grace.

Now we will conclude this general survey of the first three chapters of Genesis. We will take Genesis 1 in a more intimate way and in a bit more detail next time.

2.
Act of Creation

Now we come to a more detailed study of Genesis chapter 1. You will remember that we have studied, in a much more brief way, the first three chapters of Genesis. We have looked at the meaning of each chapter and we have found something of the Holy Spirit's purpose in giving us two accounts of creation, one in Genesis 1 and the other in Genesis 2. We have looked at some of the words used in these three chapters including the names used for God. We also looked at the words used for "to create, to make," two different words used for "to make" with a very distinct meaning. All we can simply say is that we have found that Genesis 1 deals with what we have called the fact of creation, that is, the question of the origin of creation and of humanity. From where did it come and is there a clue anywhere in the Scripture as to the method? If there is, it will be found in Genesis 1. There we have the fact of creation, where it all originated, the source behind it, and something of the method in it.

In Genesis 2, there is an entirely different structure. There the whole purpose is not the fact of creation, but the purpose of creation. Because it is the purpose of creation, it answers the question: What is the goal of creation and humanity? What is the end that is in view and why? All this is found in Genesis 2.

Then, of course, Genesis 3 deals with the explanation of the present and the answer to it. If God had this great purpose, if He brought all this into being, why is it that the whole thing seems to have broken down and collapsed and seems to be a contradiction today? Genesis 3 supplies us with the answer.

Genesis 1
  —origin of creation
  —the method
Genesis 2
  —purpose of creation
  —the goal
Genesis 3
  —the explanation of
  the present condition

We remember how we found the very, very wonderful way the Holy Spirit has used the titles, the different names for God in those three chapters. How the Holy Spirit uses one particular name in chapter 2, and in chapter 1, He uses another. He uses words that are all bound up with the purpose of each of these chapters.

Now we come to Genesis 1, and I am going to say straightway that there are a lot of difficulties in Genesis 1. I do not believe, as a child of God, that it is honouring to try to gloss over the honest difficulties that we find within the Word of God. We have to find the difficulties, acknowledge the difficulties, and go on in faith. Genesis 1 has certain difficulties. In the course of this study, we shall mention some of those difficulties. We will not be able to mention all of them, but we shall be able to mention some of them.

Four Different Views of Genesis 1

There are four different views about Genesis 1 and I want to spend just a few moments outlining those different views. They are all connected with the six days you find mentioned in Genesis 1. They are terminated by this little phrase: "And there was evening and there was morning, day one ..." There was evening and there was morning, day second, or second day, and then third day, fourth day, fifth day, and then, the sixth day.

The Unspecified Period of Time View

Around these, of course, there have come to be a multitude of interpretations. The first interpretation that we shall look at is simply that these six days are not meant to be understood in our understanding of "a day." That is a view that has been held, I suppose, for well over a thousand years in the church. In other words, these days mentioned in Genesis 1 are unspecified periods of time. In the last hundred years, people have called them geological ages. They have felt that the six days here in Genesis 1 are what is spoken of in another place, "A day with the Lord is as a thousand years and a thousand years is as a day." Particularly about 150 years or more ago, when there was so much discovery concerning the universe, there was a reaction to throw overboard the truth and the authority of the Bible. Quite a number of people tried to meet it with an apology for the Word. They sought to explain Genesis 1 as not being days as we know them. They said, "Oh, we quite agree. You have found evidence now that the creation could not have been created in one week of six days. Therefore, we believe that these days are just figurative of an unspecified time period."

Now, that presents us with some difficulties. The first is simply, what about light in verse 3 and then verse 14? Are we to understand that light was in existence without the sun and without the moon? If these are long ages of unspecified time, then evidently, quite a long period elapsed between light coming into existence and the sun coming into existence. That is one difficulty.

Another difficulty is this little phrase that re-occurs again and again through this chapter, "There was evening and there was morning." Why is this reiterated? Is it, as the people who believe in this particular view say, just poetic? Just, as it were, trying to clearly define an era of time, an epoch? Why does it say, there was an evening and a morning? As someone has pointed out, does it mean that there was a period of daylight, which perhaps covered thousands of years and then a period of night which covered thousands of years? If so, all life as we know it would have died. There are a lot of difficulties in trying to look upon this chapter as six periods of time.

Then again, there is the difficulty of the sixth day. Do we then believe that the sixth day was a geological age? What about man? Did he come into existence in the last few hours of a very long period of time? Or was he a process of evolution, slowly evolved over this period of time, who emerged, suddenly, by the Word of God at the end of it? There are some difficulties with that.

What about the seventh day of rest? Are we to believe that man was created in this sixth period and that on the seventh "day" there was a period of unspecified time of the Sabbath when nothing was done and nothing was allowed to be done, but all had to rest, including man? In this view, we would have to take the first six days as periods of time, and we would have to take the seventh day as one actual day as we know it. So there you have some more difficulties. I am not going to say anymore. I leave you with the difficulties, and I leave you with the view.

The Catastrophe View

The second view is one which was taught even as early as the church fathers, which, of course, goes right back to almost the beginning. It is what we call the *catastrophe view*. It is simply that between verse 1 and verse 2 there was a most terrible catastrophe. "In the beginning God created the heavens and the earth." People usually say here, "That means in the beginning everything was the product of God's creation. It was something that was beautiful and wonderful." Then, when we come to verse 2, "The earth was waste and void and darkness was upon the face of the earth." There have been many who felt that, between those two verses, a terrible catastrophe took place, which we discover further on in the Word of God to be the fall of the angel, the fall of Satan. This has affected the original creation of the heavens and the earth, so that the whole thing was ruined.

Now, there is a good deal more in this view than just that. We can look into it a little more carefully and see the actual words that have been used in verse 2: "The earth was waste and void." It can be translated, "without form and void; formlessness," or it can be translated "confusion" or "desolation." The other word means "emptiness." The most interesting thing is in Isaiah 45:18–19, upon which this view is built: "For thus saith Jehovah that created the heavens, the God that formed the earth and made it, that established it and created it not a waste, that formed it to be inhabited: I am Jehovah; and there is no one else. I have not spoken in secret, in a place of the land of darkness; I said not unto the seed of Jacob, Seek ye me in vain: I, Jehovah, speak righteousness, I declare things that are right."

The Lord here said, "I created it not a waste, but formed it to be inhabited." The folk who believe that there was a catastrophe between these two verses say, "The Lord definitely says to us that He did not create it to be waste." But then the other folk say, "That is exactly what He is not saying. He is saying He created it. Its waste was not His meaning. It is a means to an end."

However, the most interesting of all is found in Jeremiah 4:23–24. Now, this is very interesting because it uses exactly the same word that is used in Genesis 1:2, and Jeremiah is describing the result of sin. He says, "I beheld the earth, and, lo it was waste and void; and the heavens, and they had no light. I beheld the mountains, and, lo they trembled and all the hills moved to and fro ..." and so on. He is describing sin and judgment upon sin and he uses the very three things: waste, void, no light.

It is also interesting, and, again, people who believe in this particular view of Genesis 1 always bring this up, that God is not the author of confusion, which is the word here, "confusion." He is the God of order, not of confusion; peace and order. Second, He is not the God of emptiness. You remember in Matthew 12 the Lord Jesus gives a parable and speaks of the emptiness of a man being the very ground for evil spirits to come in. Thirdly, it says in 1 John 1:5b, "In Him there is no darkness at all." Those three things are very, very interesting and they are brought up again, and again to explain this first chapter of Genesis.

But there are quite a number of difficulties with that as well. For instance, there is no real evidence that there was such a catastrophe. Recently, that particular view has been losing ground very, very rapidly because it just cannot be found that there has been at any time such a catastrophe in the history of this present universe as we know it. So we will leave that.

The Literal View

The third view, in my estimation, scripturally, has far less difficulty than any of the others. That is simply the first feeling about this all together that the earth was created in six, literal days. That might raise a lot of difficulty in other ways, but it does not raise any difficulties scripturally, nor does it raise any difficulties spiritually. There are, of course, quite a number of things which we could question. For instance, if it was six days, then man was no sooner created than he entered into the Sabbath, which is rather remarkable. There are one or two other things about these six days that, in a moment, I shall be mentioning to you. But certainly, that view is more in keeping with the Word of God than the others.

The Narrative View

The other view is an ancient view that had been lost and has only just recently been, once again, recovered. It is that this chapter, Genesis 1, is not the record of creation, literally, in six days, but is the narrative of the creation given in six days. In other words, God revealed how the creation came into being with humanity and such, and He took six days to reveal it, and it was, in six successive stages. It was to Enoch that God revealed all this that we have in Genesis 1, and it took Him six days to reveal it. On the seventh day He made Enoch rest and He Himself rested from His work. That is an interesting view. At any rate, it has something to be said for it, in that it clears up quite a number of difficulties, but it creates one or two other difficulties. For instance, you look at it quite carefully and you will find one or two things that perhaps you had never really noted before. The first is the evenings and the mornings. You have those in verses 5, 8, 13, 19, 23, and 31. "There was evening and there was morning …" If this is the narrative of creation, then those evenings and those mornings can be taken perfectly literally. There was evening and there was morning. It is always a very wonderful thing that in the Bible, evening always comes before morning. In our reckoning, we always talk of a morning and an evening, but the Bible always speaks of an evening and a morning. There is a spiritual principle and truth embodied in that which is very wonderful. For any of you who may be going through a difficult time, evening always comes first. Day always follows night in the Scripture. That aside, that gets over that difficulty.

Does God have to rest at night? Since man, according to all these other views, was not even in existence, why did God have to have a sleep? Why did He, as it were, have to rest at night? God doesn't need to have an evening to have to refresh Himself and get back His energy again, and since man was only created on the sixth day, then why all this need about the evening? Why the stress upon the evening and the resting all the time? That is something very interesting. It says in Scripture, quite clearly, God does not slumber; He is not weary. He does not need to sleep, the Scripture quite clearly states.

Then, again, note that in verse 5 it never says, "the first day." That is how most people read it—God called the light day and the darkness He called night. And there was evening and there was morning, the first day. It does not say that. It literally is, in the Hebrew, "day one." In verse 8, it says "day second" or second day, third day, fourth day, fifth day and then a very interesting thing, "day the sixth." So it does not mean that this is the light that was the first day, it means, evidently, that it was the beginning of a series. In a particular series of six, it was day one, and then after that it was the second, the third, the fourth, the fifth, and then the sixth. That is very interesting because if it is the narrative of creation, that is perfectly in accord with that.

Then, why was there a need for a seventh day's rest as far as God was concerned? Was He tired and weary through the creation? I think that it is quite clear in the Word of God. If you look it up, Mark 2:23–27 says that the Sabbath was created for man. It was not man for the Sabbath, but the Sabbath for man. It was instituted for man's benefit and it is the evidence of God's everlasting love and care for man. The principle of the Sabbath is very interesting. You will note, of course, that if Adam had been created on the sixth day, he really had very little need to rest. He was only barely a few hours old when he had to have his first day's rest. Whereas, if this was the narrative of creation, then six whole days have gone, quite full of instruction, and there came round the day when he rested.

Then note something else which is very interesting; it is reiterated again and again, the little phrase, "God said." Just go through this first chapter and underline every time it says, God said. Now, why was God saying? Since man did not even come into being until the sixth day, what was God speaking for all the time? God said this; God said that; God said the other. Of course, we know there is a great principle behind that which we are going to draw out in a moment. Why was God speaking all the time? Even more interesting, why did it continually speak of God calling? God called this, this; and that, that. Was there any need for God to give names to things? Are we going to just take this as fellowship? God, in the Trinity, as it were, just having fellowship together, talking of these things? What really is behind this? Why did God say, "Let us make man?" It is very, very interesting.

Then, in verse 29, it says, "And God said, 'Behold I have given you every herb yielding seed which is upon the face of all the earth and every tree in which is the fruit of the tree yielding seed, to you it shall be for food. And to every beast of the earth, and to every bird of the heaven, to everything that creepeth upon the earth, wherein there is life I have given every green herb for food' and it was so. And God saw everything that He had made and behold it was very good." Now there, we all realise God was speaking to man because just a little earlier it says, "God blessed them and said unto them, 'Be fruitful.'" Why do we take verse 29 in one way and the rest of the use of "God said, God called" in another? If it is the narrative of creation, it is most instructive that God was speaking. He was instructing, He was calling this, this and that, that. It was as if He had man before Him and He has got in hand, as it were, his education. There again, it is very, very interesting.

Now, of course, there are difficulties to this view, which is why we cannot, with great joy and dogmatism, say, "This is it." The difficulties are, of course, found in Genesis 2:1–3, "And the heavens and the earth were finished, and all the host of them. And on the seventh day God finished His work which He had made; and He rested on the seventh day from all His work which He had made. And God blessed the seventh day, and hallowed it; because in it He rested from all the work which God had created and made." That, of course, is quoted in Exodus 20:6–11, in Exodus 31:14–15, in Hebrews 4:4 and quite a few other places in the Word. It would seem to suggest that God made the heavens and the earth in six days.

The interesting thing is that the little word "made" is the word *asah*, which is used 2,500 times in the Old Testament. It is the word in Scripture which has the greatest latitude of meaning and its meaning can only be determined by its context. What was God doing in the six days? Its meaning in this context determines its meaning in this particular phrase. In six days, God made.

On the seventh day God finished the work that He had made and rested on the seventh day from all His work which He had made. God blessed it. Wiseman says here that he would put it this way: he would have put the word "did," "to do," not necessarily meaning the creation that was in view, but the narrative. It was the work that was in view. God did something in six days and He finished it on the sixth day, and desisted, ceased from it on the seventh. Wiseman says that if you take that every time it comes up, you find it definitely does fit in. I have looked through them all, and looked them all up, and he is certainly right. It is quite possible to take that as the meaning in Exodus 20, in Exodus 31, and in Hebrew 4:4. You can definitely understand it as meaning that God did something in six days and He ceased from it on the seventh day.

Well, there has been a tremendous amount of controversy about those chapters. One very interesting thing emerges— Genesis 1 to Genesis 2:4 is the most ancient form of Hebrew poetry. (You remember we spoke of this last time.) It is called parallelism. It has an introduction, and the key to the parallel, in Genesis 1:1–2. Then you have three days and, paralleled with the three days, a second series of three days. Then you have a conclusion and a colophon, which was the ancient literary method giving the date, the title, and the author. That is in chapter 2, verse 4: "These are the generations ..." This word "generations" is *toledoth* in the Hebrew. It just means "history." The Septuagint translates it quite clearly: "the book of the history of the heavens and the earth when they were created in the day that the Lord God made heaven and earth." The Lord God is the author, the date is when He gave this revelation, and the title is "The Book of the History of the Heavens and the Earth."

Here you have, in day one, light, just generally, and in the fourth day you have the lights, which corresponds to light. The second day you have water and atmosphere, and in the fifth day you have life in the water and life in the atmosphere. The third day you have land and vegetation, and the sixth day, which corresponds to it, you have animals and man. You have the key to the parallelism, "without form," and you have form coming into being, as it were. You have "empty;" and then fullness in the emptiness. Something at any rate to investigate, isn't it? It is very, very interesting.

This view gets over a tremendous number of difficulties of how there was light long before the sun came. Whether it is the narrative of creation, about one thing we can be clear: the first chapter is in poetic form. In it may well be the key to our understanding of it.

Note: Hebrew Literary Method in Genesis 1:1–2:4
Parallelism—a form of poetry
- Introduction
- Three thoughts compared
- Conclusion
- Colophon–ending statement of date, title, and author

Introduction: Genesis 1:1–2	
Comparing Thoughts: Genesis 1:3–1:31	
Separating:	**Filling with:**
Day 1: Light/Dark	Day 4: Sun/Moon/Stars
Day 2: Water/Sky	Day 5: Fish/Birds
Day 3: Water/Land	Day 6: Plants/Animals/Land
Conclusion: Genesis 2:1–3	
Colophon: Genesis 2:4	
Author: *Jehovah*	
Date: When He gave the Revelation	
Title: *The Book of the History of the Heavens and the Earth*	

The Sovereign Activity of God

Now we will get away from what seems to be so dry. What conclusion can we come to over Genesis 1? The first thing is that creation is the result of the sovereign activity of God. If you look at Genesis 1, verse 1: "In the beginning God ..." That is, it all begins with God. You can never get beyond that fact; it is written from beginning to end of the Bible. This little phrase comes up again and again: "The Lord, that made heaven and earth ..." It was sovereign activity.

You know, the little phrase, "In the beginning God ..." contains within it oh, so much. What was there in the beginning? We know there was the Trinity, the triune God in a fellowship of love and inter-communion and inter-dependence. We know that. "In the beginning God."

Another thing we know is that there was a tremendous purpose formed in the heart of God from before the foundation of the world, and all the sovereign activity, as far as creation goes, came out of that purpose in God. It is something very, very wonderful.

In the beginning, the cross was foreordained, a lamb slain from the foundation of the world. That was in the beginning. That found its rise in the heart of God. It was no mere happening. It was no after thought of God's. It was no swiftly engineered answer to meet the situation. In the beginning, God had planned the lamb slain.

Furthermore, you find the church in that first few words, "In the beginning God ..." That is where you find the church. I know that might bring difficulties again about our free will and everything else, but there is one thing that is absolutely clear: that the beginning of the church is in God. It begins with God. In Him it took its rise. In Him it, as it were, was conceived. Out of Him it was brought forth. It is one of those great thoughts of God: the church. "In the beginning God."

The first conclusion we can come to about Genesis 1 is that creation is the outcome of the sovereign activity of God.

We shall look at method in a moment, but it began with God. It was sovereign activity.

The Word of God

The second thing we want to note is that creation is by the Word of God. Putting aside all these different, conflicting views, one thing emerges very, very clearly: this whole natural creation came by the Word of God. He spoke and it was done.

Hebrews 11:3: "By faith we understand that the world has been framed by the Word of God so that what is seen has not been made out of things which appear." One thing we get very clearly is that the creation is by the Word of God.

Second Peter 3:5: "For this they wilfully forget, that there were heavens from of old and an earth compacted out of water and amidst water, by the word of God." Then compare that with verse 7: "But the heavens that now are and the earth, by the same word have been stored up for fire." Everything is by the Word of God.

If we first get it absolutely clear that Genesis 1 teaches us that creation is the result of the sovereign activity of God, the second thing we learn is that creation is by the very Word of God. You will find that right through the Word—the power of the Word of God. It is the most wonderful thing to sit back and meditate upon. I know there are many who have very real difficulties, but when a person has been saved and can believe in the incarnation, and then in the resurrection, and they have experienced new birth by the Spirit of God, is it a harder thing to believe that this whole creation is here by the Word of God?

It is very clearly stated in II Corinthians 4 that it is a harder thing—if anything, certainly no easier—for God to create a heaven and earth than to bring someone into the new creation. It is contrasted with that very thing: "God, who commanded light to shine out of darkness, hath shined into our hearts." The same Word of God, which brought all into being, is the agent by which a man or a woman is converted. Faith cometh by hearing and hearing by the Word of God. Isn't that wonderful?

I don't think we put enough upon God's Word because the Word of God lies behind everything. I do not have to point out to you that every single move in the history of humanity has begun with the Word of God. Whether it has been right back in the beginning, when He called everything into existence and created it all, or whether it was the creation of humanity, or whether it was Noah. It was by the Word of God that God appeared to him, spoke to him. We have an ark. Or whether it was Abraham: The God of glory appeared unto our father Abraham and spoke and told him to get out. "Get thee out." It was by the Word of God that a new movement in the history of God's dealings with men was brought into being.

Moses, is another remarkable example of the Word of God, "I AM that I AM. Go and say I AM has sent you." It was the Word of God. It is the same if you want the Ten Commandments, if you want the Tabernacle, God's dwelling place amongst men, but supremely with the Lord Jesus. He is the Word of God. Thus, you see, all things are by the Word of God. That is the second thing we learn about creation. It is by the Word of God.

Creation Made Through and For the Lord Jesus

The third thing we learn about creation is that it was made through the Lord Jesus and for the Lord Jesus. That is a very, very important thing and it is the key to the whole question.

In the beginning was the Word, and the Word was with God and the Word was God. The same was in the beginning with God. All things were made through him; and without him was not anything made that hath been made. (John 1:1–3)

For in Him were all things created, in the heaven and upon earth, things visible and things invisible, whether thrones or dominions or principalities or powers; all things have been created through him and unto him. (Colossians 1:16)

Yet to us there is one God, the Father, of whom are all things, and we unto him; and one Lord, Jesus Christ, through whom are all things, and we through him. (1 Corinthians 8:6)

… hath at the end of these days spoken unto us in his Son, whom he appointed heir of all things, through whom also he made the worlds … (Hebrews 1:2)

Thus, the third thing we can learn is that the whole of creation was made through the Lord Jesus Christ. He was there. It was through Him that it was all created and He was the goal of it. That is most important. It was for Him; through Him and for Him.

Creation's Agent: The Spirit of God

The fourth thing we learn about creation is in Genesis 1:2: "The Spirit of God brooded upon the waters." The Spirit of God moved upon the face of the waters. The word is "fluttered," or "hovered" or "brooded" upon the face of the waters.

You come now to a very, very important point. The creation was the result of the sovereign activity of God. It was by the Word of God. It was through the Lord Jesus and for the Lord Jesus. Now we come to the Holy Spirit and we link three things: the Word of God, the Lord Jesus, and the Holy Spirit. We must link those three in creation, for the Spirit of God is always the agent of creation. Indeed, the Holy Spirit is always the agent in any creative activity of God. Always. If it is through the Lord Jesus and for the Lord Jesus, the Holy Spirit is always the agent. Thus, you see, the Lord Jesus coming into this earth was by the Spirit of God. He was conceived by the Holy Spirit. He was baptised, as it were, into His ministry in the Holy Spirit, the water yes, but it was the Holy Spirit that came upon Him for the ministry, for His service. It was by the eternal Spirit that He offered Himself up to God on the cross and it was by the Spirit that He was raised: "The Spirit of Him that raised up Christ Jesus from the dead ..."

How was the church created? Through Christ and for Christ. But who is the agent? The Holy Spirit at Pentecost. When the Holy Spirit was come, the church was come. The church was in the Holy Spirit and the Holy Spirit is the agent. It is not only naturally that the Holy Spirit is the agent of creation, but also spiritually. The third person of the Trinity is the agent of all the creative activity of God wherever you find God at work.

The Necessity of Faith

Then, the last thing, the conclusion that we can come to about this first chapter is found in a verse we have already read in Hebrews 11:3. It is the absolute necessity of faith. "By faith we understand that the worlds have been framed by the Word of God, so that what is seen hath not been made out of things which appear."

I do feel that we make our greatest mistake in getting onto ground that is too apologetic. We are all the time defending, all the time apologising, all the time trying to meet continual criticism from different quarters. We cannot do it. When we are on the defensive, we generally lose ground anyway. You see, it is by faith we understand. Whereas human knowledge is changing all the time, and as it were, finding that it was wrong so many years ago and having to modify its views, indeed sometimes having to leave old ground altogether, the Word of God has never yet been proved wrong. Though it has been contradicted quite openly, quite dogmatically, categorically, in the end it has always come out on top. So it is by real faith, not stupid faith. I mean that kind of stupidity that some people consider to be faith. By real, genuine faith, which is the gift of God, we understand that the worlds were framed by the Word of God. That is the attitude with which to come to Genesis 1. It may have many difficulties. Those difficulties may have been placed there by the Holy Spirit with the very reason of drawing out faith in us. We just have to take the ground of clear-cut faith with God in the whole question of the Word of God. It is not just something which is purely rational, purely logical, the answer to everything found everywhere. It is not that at all. We have to come to the Word of God by faith and by faith we understand that the worlds were framed by the Word of God and the things which have been made which are seen have been made from what does not appear. That I say is very, very wonderful.

Creation as a Gradual Process

Now, having got clearly into our minds and hearts that it is God's work and the sovereign activity of God, let us have a look at Genesis 1 a little more closely. The first thing I want you to note is the possibility of a gradual process. This is very interesting. Now, I do not want you to think that I am trying to apologise for anything. I am looking at the Word of God itself and the meaning of the very words the Holy Spirit has used. There is, within the first chapter of Genesis, the possibility of a gradual process. Genesis 1:9: "God said, 'Let the waters under the heavens be gathered together unto one place and let the dry land appear.'" There is the possibility of a process there—the waters being gathered and the dry land appearing.

Then again, look at verse 11: "God said, 'Let the earth put forth grass, herb yielding seed and fruit trees bearing fruit.'" Now, we cannot say it in good English, but the word here is: "God said, 'Let the earth be caused to sprout, or caused to germinate.'" The idea is that, by the Word of God, forces were let loose in the earth which somehow germinated things. Things started to sprout. Here is a possibility of a process. We have got to get clear. Do we believe that God stood, as He well could, and said, "Let this be," and it immediately happened there? Fully grown trees, fully grown plants, fully grown animals, birds, fish, all just there suddenly? Well, I believe that God is perfectly able to do that. It is not beyond His power; He is perfectly able to do it. But what does the Word of God say? It suggests a process. "God said," and what did He say? What happened? It all began with the Word of God. But what was the method? It is very interesting. Let the earth be caused to sprout—vegetation, herb, fruit trees.

Look at verse 20: "God said, 'Let the waters swarm with swarms of living creatures.'" Again, the word is simply, "Let the waters be caused to swarm." Forces let loose by the Word of God and something happening in the very waters.

Then verse 24: "God said, 'Let the earth bring forth ...'" Do you see how God spoke? "Let the earth bring forth," not "I put on the earth." "Let the earth bring forth." Something was caused to come out of the earth. Well, what came out of the earth? We read here living creatures after their kind, cattle, and creeping things. Isn't that interesting? They came out of the earth.

Genesis 2:5: "No plant of the field was yet in the earth. No herb of the field was yet sprung up ..." Do you see that? "For the Lord God had not caused it to rain upon the earth and there was not a man to till the ground. But there went up a mist from the earth and watered the whole face of the ground." So evidently, all this vegetable life, as it were, was waiting for rain. It was going to spring up according to a method. That is very, very wonderful.

Genesis 2:8: "The Lord God planted a garden, eastward in Eden and there He put the man whom He had formed." God planted the garden. There is the possibility of a process. Verse 9: "And out of the ground made the Lord God to grow every tree that is pleasant for sight and good for food." Again, you have the possibility of a process, of a gradual process.

Now, let's be quite unbiased as we come to the Word of God in this way, and see what the Word of God itself teaches us here. What I do want you to notice is that the word "to create," *bara*, in Hebrew, is always used of the sovereign activity of God, that is, it was a new thing. It comes in verse 1, at the beginning of all existence, verse 20, at the beginning of animate life, and then again in verse 27, the beginning of human life. What we learn by this is simply that behind it all is the sovereign activity of God. The method may, in some cases, be a method of process, gradual process, but in every instance it goes back to the Word of God, and behind the Word of God, the sovereignty of God Himself. That is very, very important to learn.

God is Light

Now let's just look together at some of these verses. First, let's look together at Genesis 1:3–5. You see from these verses that God said that He commanded the light to be. It is interesting in II Corinthians 4:6 it says: "God commanded light to shine out of darkness." The suggestion in the Word of God is that light was always there. It was something that was brought into manifestation, rather than existence. Some energy, some force which, as it were, was being manifested as light. This you will find throughout the Word. I have found nowhere in the Word, where it says light was created. It always speaks of light being brought out, as it were, into visibility, if you want to put it that way, being manifested. "Let light be." That is how the Hebrew puts it. "Let light be and light was." Second Corinthians 4:6 says, "God commanded light to shine out of darkness."

Now, I expect most of you know, better than I do, that light, heat, electricity, galvanism, are all different manifestations of one basic force, or one basic energy. There is one basic energy behind them all and there are different manifestations. I believe that the Word of God teaches quite simply that God is that energy. Where it refers to God as light, it does not only mean spiritual light, though primarily it refers to spiritual light. God is light. The Lord Jesus said, "I am the light of the world."

It is interesting that there is coming a day when there will be no need of the sun or the moon, as we know it. That is going to be abolished. It says quite expressly that the Lord God and the Lamb are going to be the light thereof. In other words, there is going to come a day, when this energy, in some way, is going to be used in another manifestation. We are going to have light, but somehow or other, it is not going to need the sun or the moon, as we know it. It is extremely interesting. It is rather wonderful, I think, to investigate that more deeply: the whole question of what this basic, elementary energy is out of which everything has come into existence. I am afraid that I am not skilled enough, nor intelligent enough to be able to speak about that well enough.

However, there is one thing we do know, and that is that right at the heart of everything created, whether visible or invisible—and remember, there are many things created that are not visible—there is a basic energy or life which, as it were, finds its manifestation in many different ways. I understand that our very bodies are but the manifestation of that basic energy. If we could only see it, we are, I understand, so many little particles hanging together in some way or another—just an expression of energy. Everything that we see is just the same. Now, the Word of God clearly tells us that in Him all things hold together or consist. He is the energy of which all this is just an expression— even furnishings, *everything* is purely just an expression of an energy. Now, Paul says, "In Him we live and move and have our being." Long before all this was discovered as such, he said, "In Him," that is God, "we live," and then speaking to unsaved people, "we live, we move, we have our being." That is, unsaved people live in God, move in God, as such, and have their being in God. That is the amazing thing. It is what this twentieth century has forgotten. It is totally absent in the preaching of the gospel, that however ungodly you are, you are there by the grace of God. Your very body is just a manifestation of God's life, perverted maybe, distorted maybe, fallen maybe, but there it is. You understand the wrath of God and, one day, those who have been so arrogant, presumptuous, and conceited, will be dealt with by the righteous judgment of God. So, you see, there is something that is very, very, *very* wonderful. It requires as much power to shine in our hearts as it did to bring light out of darkness.

Another thing I understand is that light needs an organ that is capable of receiving it. We have a wonderful organ in our human eye. It is built in such a way as to be capable of receiving the light. If something happens to my eye, I can be surrounded by light and live in darkness. What a lesson that is for us with the Lord! Something goes wrong with our spiritual eye, the organ that the Holy Spirit has given us for seeing God who dwelleth in light that is unapproachable, seeing the Lord, and even in the midst of light we can grope in darkness. We do not see anything. There is a blind spot in our eye. It reveals a lot when we talk about the speck in someone else's eye and we have got the beam in our own. It is terrible, but just simply means we cannot see the light. Something has happened to our eye. How important it is, just to see that spiritual organ, unimpaired, working properly.

I understand that the world is full of light, potential or existent. That is, it is there potentially or it is there in actual existence. So there, I think, is something very, very wonderful indeed. The Scripture calls us sons of the light and of the day. That, of course, is spiritually speaking. But it is a wonderful thing that God always associates dark with night and light with day. That is, we are sons of the light and sons of the day.

Light has a tremendous importance in the Word of God. You have only to look at the Psalms to see the importance that light plays, they are frequently speaking of light. The Scripture always speaks of light as embodied in God.

There are many other things that we could say, things that I have read and things that I have been told about light, which I think we will have to leave. But there is something in this for your investigation anyway. The whole point is that light, as far as I can see it, is but a manifestation of that energy which is the very life of God Himself. What a wonderful thing that is!

3.
Purpose of Creation

Genesis 2:5–25

And no plant of the field was yet in the earth, and no herb of the field had yet sprung up; for Jehovah God had not caused it to rain upon the earth: and there was not a man to till the ground; but there went up a mist from the earth, and watered the whole face of the ground. And Jehovah God formed man of the dust of the ground, and breathed into his nostrils the breath of life; and man became a living soul. And Jehovah God planted a garden eastward, in Eden; and there he put the man whom he had formed. And out of the ground made Jehovah God to grow every tree that is pleasant to the sight, and good for food; the tree of life also in the midst of the garden, and the tree of the knowledge of good and evil. And a river went out of Eden to water the garden; and from thence it was parted, and became four heads. The name of the first is Pishon: that is it which compasseth the whole land of Havilah, where there is gold; and the gold of that land is good: there is bdellium and the onyx stone. And the name of the second river is Gihon: the same is it that compasseth the whole land of Cush. And the name of the third river is Hiddekel: that is it which goeth in front of Assyria. And the fourth river is the Euphrates. And Jehovah God took the man, and put him into the garden of Eden to dress it and to keep it. And Jehovah God commanded the man, saying, Of every tree of the garden thou mayest freely eat: but of the tree of the knowledge of good and evil, thou shalt not eat of it: for in the day that thou eatest thereof thou shalt surely die.

And Jehovah God said, It is not good that the man should be alone; I will make him a help meet for him. And out of the ground Jehovah God formed every beast of the field, and every bird of the heavens; and brought them unto the man to see what he would call them: and whatsoever the man called every living creature, that was the name thereof. And the man gave names to all cattle, and to the birds of the heavens, and to every beast of the field; but for man there was not found a help meet for him. And Jehovah God caused a deep sleep to fall upon the man, and he slept; and he took one of his ribs, and closed up the flesh instead thereof: and the rib, which Jehovah God had taken from the man, made he a woman, and brought her unto the man. And the man said, This is now bone of my bones, and flesh of my flesh: she shall be called Woman, because she was taken out of Man. Therefore shall a man leave his father and *his mother, and shall cleave unto his wife: and they shall be one flesh. And they were both naked,* *the man and his wife, and were not ashamed.*

We come now to this second chapter of Genesis. We remember that the verses up to verse 4, really belong to the first chapter and that chapter 2 really begins with verse 5. Whilst I think Genesis 1 is tremendously instructive and informative, Genesis 2 is vital. I do not suppose there is one of us, including myself, in this room that really recognises just how vital this second chapter of Genesis is. If we had not received it, we should quite honestly not understand that one of the real foundation stones of the whole Bible would be missing. When we came to Genesis 3, we wouldn't really know what it was about if Genesis 3 followed straight on from Genesis 1. This chapter is absolutely vital. I do believe, that if the Lord would really open it up to us in a new way and give us a real inward understanding of what is here within this passage, it would probably give a different complexion to our own lives.

One of our greatest needs is the understanding of what we are. Of course, to understand what we have become is a very, very great need. To understand what God meant us to be is just as important. We are going to understand first what God originally intended. That is very, very important. What did God originally intend in man? What kind of man did He intend? What constitution did that man have? As what, did He first form him? What was he like? We will find out, secondly, what has happened. Why are we like we are; quite different? We are a wholly different species to what God first created, quite different. Then we need to understand, thirdly, what is happening to us now that we have come to the Lord. Those three things are very, very important to our understanding, in fact, to the whole question of our salvation, and indeed, of the church because it is all here within this passage.

The Creation of Man

You remember what we said about Genesis 1. We found there that man was the apex or the climax of creation. He was the crown of creation or the consummation of God's work. God, began with some of the simplest and the most profound things, and gradually he built up a creation, layer after layer, foundation after foundation. Gradually, the whole of creation unfolds in vista after vista and, in the end, He crowns it all with man. It is quite obvious in Genesis 1 that man is absolutely unique and is the consummation of all God's work. He is the crown. He is the top stone of the whole structure. That is how we left it last time.

When you come to Genesis 2, you find something quite different. Man is not the crown; man is the beginning. Man is not the top stone; he is the foundation. Man is, as it were, the beginning of everything and he is the centre of everything. That has led some people, quite falsely, to say that the second chapter of Genesis is an altogether different account of creation, that you have here two accounts of creation, which wholly contradict one another. If you want to look at it from that point of view, there is a lot to be said in its favour. I could spend most of this evening pointing out to you things which would seem to be gross contradiction to Genesis 1, if you want to read it like that. For instance, it quite expressly says in chapter 2 that man came before any plants or any birds or anything else. Man was the first thing. God made man and then all the rest flowed out after man. He made the plants and the herbs and the trees and the garden. We find the animals and the birds all come later, whereas in Genesis 1 it all comes before. You see also the name of God is different in the second chapter of Genesis. The name here used is *Jehovah*, whereas in the first chapter of Genesis it is *Elohim*. They said, therefore, that Moses brought two contradictory accounts. They often say the second one, in Genesis 2, is the earliest and the most ancient. The other, in Genesis 1, is a more recent one and he has done a very bad job in editing them. He has brought them together in a very, very poor way indeed.

Well, I think, really, we shall find the answer quite clearly. Of course, apart from anything else, even if there is no such thing as inspiration and Moses was not led of the Holy Spirit, it would still be quite stupid to believe that view because we know, we understand that Moses was a very highly educated and cultured man. I just cannot for a moment, even on human and rational grounds, conceive of a man bringing two documents together in such a terrible way. He leaves the most gross contradictions, side by side almost. It is absolutely pure stupidity, how people with minds and intelligences and understanding of Hebrew could possibly, really hold such views. It is in itself evidence of the amazing power of the enemy's deception to be able to do it. Moses, as you know, was brought up in Pharaoh's court, son of Pharaoh's daughter, given every kind of advantage in education, in upbringing, in social standard, and in everything else. Josephus informs us that he was a man, mighty not only in strength and valour, but in mind. He was a man who, according to Josephus at any rate, left his mark upon even the Egypt of his generation.

So, even from that point of view, it is obvious to us that there is a reason why there are these two accounts. However, we have something far, far more wonderful—we know that the Bible has been written by the Holy Spirit. Therefore, we have to find out why the Holy Spirit has now brought in a second account of creation which is so totally different in complexion to the first.

I do not think the answer is really very far from us. The key to the whole problem is something that we have already said. Genesis 2 is the *purpose* of creation. Genesis 1 is the *fact* of creation, that is, how did it happen? Out of what did it come? Where did it begin? How? Was there any method of creation that we can define, any method that we can see, if only dimly, that God used? Well, if you are going to find any method at all, do not look for it in Genesis 2 because you will not find it. If there is method for all creative acts, it is in Genesis 1. If there is an order, should we say an historic order for all created things, you will find it in Genesis 1. Genesis 1 is the fact of creation.

Genesis 2 is the purpose of creation. Why? For what reason? Where is it all going? What is the goal of creation? In Genesis 1, we have the fact of it all. God, has revealed to us how the whole thing came into being, but why? Why go to all this trouble? Why bring all this into being? What is the reason? Genesis 2 is the purpose of creation. Simply, to put it in a few words: man

A Comparison of the Creation Accounts

Genesis 1	Genesis 2
Notes historical order with hints of the method of creation	No timeline of creation is expressed
Notes the facts of creation	Notes the purpose of creation–the "why"
God is known as Elohim	God is known as Jehovah
Context is clear and simple	Context is figurative and an amplification of Genesis 1

Genesis 1 shows man as the climax

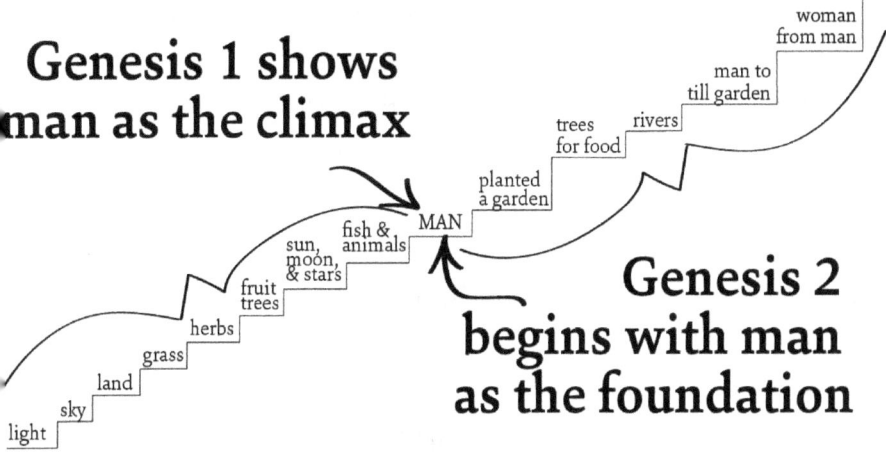

woman from man

man to till garden

trees for food

rivers

planted a garden

fish & animals

MAN

sun, moon, & stars

fruit trees

herbs

grass

land

sky

light

Genesis 2 begins with man as the foundation

was made by God, for God. Now, that is a very simple statement, but that simple statement is the key to everything. Man was made *by* God, *for* God. If you would look deeply into that, it is this that we find very hard to believe, even as children of God. We believe it in the mind; we do not believe it as experience. We have this inbred idea that we have been made for other things. We have either been made for this life, or made for one another, or made for all kinds of things. We cannot grasp the simple key to the whole problem of humanity, which is that humanity was made primarily for God. Oh, if we could only grasp that! If the Holy Spirit could only bring that into our minds and our hearts, it would solve so many of our problems.

Our problems are all to do with this simple thought of for what reason we are made. We just cannot believe that we were made for God. In Genesis 2, it just says simply, beautifully, clearly, man was made for God. Man is a vessel made for God, a being capable of holding God. As such, he can never get anywhere and be satisfied, or do anything really until he fulfils the function for which he was created. We have to realise that, in creation, everything had a purpose. It was all there with a function, with an order.

Man had an amazing dual function. He had a function, first of all, which was earthward. He was, in that sense, the crown of creation. He was the top, the top stone really. Do you see what I mean? He brought everything up in one great swooping to himself and became in one moment the height and the glory of creation. He was the most unique climax of it all. But from that point, man has another function, which the rest of creation does not have, which goes up to God. He has that dual function, in which he brings the whole of creation together in himself as the apex, the top stone, and then he brings all of God down to a point into this earth. It is a most amazing dual function that man has.

Primarily, man was made for God; let us get that clear. Now, of course, Satan has done a most amazing work and left us as, what Jude called, sensual beings, that is creatures, animals, just pure animals. We have lost our function God-ward and we now are just creatures that really are perverted, like a bird with broken wings. It was meant to fly, but it cannot fly. All it can do is drag its broken wings around with it, and that is humanity. In that poor, broken state of failure, it is trying to somehow satisfy itself and grovel around. Trying somehow, in its deceived self, to find what is the satisfying answer.

So the key to this second chapter of Genesis is the purpose of God, the purpose of creation. That purpose is simply bound up in an inexplicable way with man himself. I do not think it is going too far to say that man is the purpose of creation. Of course, we know the Lord Jesus is the supreme and primary cause of creation. However, I believe that man was, in the thought of God, never apart from Christ. From the very beginning, man was always seen as the complement of Christ. I do not believe for a moment that God ever thought of man as outside of that sphere. He saw him from the beginning as the complement of Christ. You have it in this second chapter of Genesis. You have the tree of life in the midst of the garden and you have this whole question of marriage. You have the whole basic meaning of God in this creation of man, of this whole order. It was that man should, with God, move on into all the fullness of God.

The Relationships of Man

You will note, I think, three things about this chapter, before we look at it in a more detailed way. First, you will see that this whole chapter is to do with the place of man and his relationships. First of all, it is the relationship of man to the Lord God. The Lord God is the Father of man's spirit and the creator of his soul—the relationship of man to God. That is why Adam is called the son of God, not a creation of God. He was the creation of God, his body was the creation of God, his soul was the creation of God. But God was his Father, in that God produced him by breathing something of Himself into him. Man was conceived in a most remarkable way. God breathed into his nostrils the breath of life. That was not a creation. That was something of God going into man and forming a link, a unity between God and man, which can only be likened to father and son. Thus, you have the relationship there of the Lord God and man.

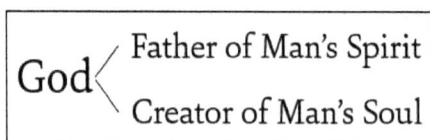

$$\boxed{\text{God}\begin{cases} \text{Father of Man's Spirit} \\ \text{Creator of Man's Soul} \end{cases}}$$

You have the relationship, also, to the tree of life. You will see that much in this chapter is to do with the tree of life. It is in the midst of the garden. Adam, later on, is told quite clearly that he must not take of the tree of the knowledge of good and evil, but the tree of life is evidently open for his coming. That is very interesting, and we shall see a little later that the relationship of man to the tree of life is set forth here. He has a relationship to it. Whatever the tree of life stands for symbolically, man has a relationship to that. It is in the midst of the garden. It is not over in a corner of the garden. It is not hidden away. It is right in the midst. It is evidently in God's thought, the very centre of the garden, something of supreme importance, in the midst of the garden. Where the tree of the knowledge of good and evil is, we are not told. It just says, "... and the tree of the knowledge of good and evil." It may have been in some pokey part of the garden, some hole in the garden, some corner of the garden. But the tree of life was right in the midst, in a central place in the midst. Straightway man's relationship to the tree of life that stands forth symbolically is set forth.

Then again, another thing you will find in here is man's relationship to the vegetable creation, or however you like to call it. For those of you who do not like gardening, man has a tremendous relationship to the natural creation. That is why so often, a person with nervous disorders is told straightway, "You must take up gardening. Get into something to do with gardening." It is the most remarkable thing that nervous disorder cases are often told, and you will laugh about this probably, either to do gardening or to keep pets. Although it may seem very odd to you and old maidish in some ways, yet, you know, it is not. There is something that goes right back to the second chapter of Genesis.

You see man's first relationship to the natural creation is a very, very wonderful link. He was put within the garden to till it and to keep it. His place was cultivation. He was to cultivate it. He was to train the plants. He was, I suppose, to find out the very sort of laws that governed these things and then to adapt himself to them and to use them and to cultivate them. Man's relationship to the natural creation is very, very interesting.

You will also see man's relationship to the animal creation here. He is the one who called them by their very names. Again, you have a very close link between man and the animal creation. Evidently, he was there, in some way, to subdue, the Word says. I suppose that is to tame, to reign in, to discipline. Because things are without sin does not mean that they do not need discipline, or cultivation, or subduing. They may well need those very things to produce something even more wonderful just because of cultivation and discipline.

You see man and his relationship to woman is also in Genesis 2. The whole relationship of man to woman is set forth quite clearly.

You have man in all his relationships in this second chapter of Genesis. Man is given a central place, right at the heart of the whole thing. Everything is centred upon and in that man and his relationships. As I have said, the man has a dual function. Evidently, his relationships in one direction are out earthward and man, as the top stone and the consummation of the whole natural creation, gives order to it all. Thus, you see, if anything happens to man, something happens to the whole of creation, not only to the natural creation, but to the animal creation. Something goes wrong if man loses his place of dominion, of government, being at the top of it all, as it were, summing it all up in himself. But even more important is his function God-ward. His relationship to the Lord God and to the tree of life is the key to his relationship to everything else. If man is wrong with the Lord God and the tree of life, then he is wrong with the natural creation, he is wrong with the animal creation, and he is wrong in his own domestic relationships. Everything goes wrong if man is out of gear there. So you see, the place of man is very, very important in this chapter.

The Figurative Nature of Genesis Two

I want you to notice that chapter 2 has a figurative nature. That is quite clear. I know some may wonder what I am getting at here, but the second chapter of Genesis has a figurative nature. There is nothing whatsoever in Genesis 1 which has a figurative nature. It is all clear-cut and simple. However, Genesis 2 has about it all the far-eastern imagery. It is speaking almost from the beginning in figure. It pays no heed to the historic order. It pays very little heed to that side at all. The whole of this chapter is fitting four things into the form and you have it again and again. These four things are the tree of life, the tree of the knowledge of good and evil, the rivers, mighty rivers, that flow up to almost the four corners of the earth and then there is this little phrase which has bewildered so many people: "... gold, bdellium, and the onyx stone ..." What is this talking about? Why is that here in this chapter?

Then Eden itself. No one knows where Eden is. There has been a tremendous amount of conjecture as to where Eden is. I suppose that upon nothing else has there been quite so much variety of view than as to where Eden is. Some people put it right over the Ganges, some have put it up in the steppes of Russia, other people have thought it right over into Turkey, and other people have put it down in Arabia. Some have gone farther afield. Oh, it is amazing if you try to find the views of the Fathers and the Reformers and others. Where was Eden? But Eden itself has one simple meaning.

It means "delight." There you have got the key to it all. God never meant us to spend hours, and hours, and hours, trying to decide exactly where Eden was. Eden has a meaning and the tree of life has a meaning. Go look for the tree of life today. You will not find it amongst the trees; neither will you find the tree of the knowledge of good and evil.

The far-eastern imagery has always passed from the real to the symbolic so easily and back again. That is what has always befuddled the western world. They cannot quite understand. We in the West are very clear you see. If we are going to talk in nice, fairy-like language, we are quite clear that everything is ridiculous. Look at Hans Andersen's fairy tales. From the beginning you see beasts turn into women and women turn into beasts and houses vanish and things like that. But the audience knows that everything is so real, and then suddenly you have gone into symbolism and that confuses them. Then you are back again into reality and then you are back again into symbolism. So you go backwards and forwards, alternating in a way that we in the West are far too taped and analytical to allow. Either you have got to be that or this. But no, here you have something, which, in its very nature, is symbolical and we have to understand that if we are going to understand Genesis 2.

An Amplification in Genesis Two

The third thing may seem to contradict what I have said. Genesis 2 is, in many ways, an amplification of Genesis 1. Whilst it speaks in a symbolical way, there are parts of it which amplify what we find in Genesis 1. For instance, there is no mention of rain in Genesis 1 and, yet, we have rain mentioned here in Genesis 2 and it is a very necessary function. No mention of mists or dew, and yet here we have the mists or the dew distinctly mentioned. We have no mention of the creation and the constitution of man in a more detailed way; here we have a very full account of the creation and the constitution of man. In Genesis 1 we are just told, "... male and female created He them." But here, we have a quite long and detailed account of the creation of woman. So you see that, in many ways, Genesis 2 amplifies quite a lot of Genesis 1.

Then I want you to notice something else about this second chapter. I want you to mark how wonderfully instructive, in the light of all I have said, is the very vocabulary of Genesis 2. Even here in your English version, if you read it carefully, as compared to Genesis 1, you will be amazed at its vocabulary. It is so different; the very words used are different. They feel different. The whole background of the words used is different to Genesis 1.

Let's take a few of them. We have already mentioned that all of these words suggest purpose and destiny. For instance, the very first thing you come across is "the Lord God". Up to now, there has been no mention of the Lord God, but now we come to Jehovah God and immediately, what does that put into view? It brings into view God in His covenant relationship with His people. Here God is found, not as the mighty God of creation and of omnipotence, but here you find God in His intimate, personal yearning to find a dwelling place in His people, to be able to walk amongst them and live in them and they in Him, becoming, as it were, a unity. You have that straightway in verse 5 and a number of other verses.

Then in verse 7, verse 8, and verse 19 you have the little word "to form," which means, as I think I have already mentioned, "to fashion" as the potter does the clay; "to constitute, to plan" is its root meaning, or even "pre-ordain." The Arabic form today is covenant or contract. So, you see, God does not create man and He does not make man. He forms man, and the whole thought behind it is a forming of the mind, a forming with an end in view, a forming with a covenant in view, a forming as it were, according to a contract that God has made. God has a great purpose in this man. Everything is formed, it even talks of the animals being formed out of the ground. It all has a purpose in it.

Then you will find another word in verse 22: "And out of the rib He made woman." This word is not the ordinary word we have mentioned so often "to make," but it is the phrase "to build up". Out of this rib, He "builded up," He "built up." We have it in the New Testament in its form "to edify, to build up." He "builded up" the woman. There is a plan behind it; there is a purpose behind it. He did not just make, the simple word, but He had a plan in mind.

In verse 8, you have the word "planted." That is a suggestive word. In Genesis 1 God caused to sprout. He caused to grow. He caused to germinate. You do not find the word "planted." Here, God planted, which, again, suggests a purpose in His mind.

In verse 8, 10, and 15, you have the word "a garden". You do not get the suggestion of a garden in chapter one, but a garden always suggests a mind, doesn't it? In fact, I am often told that a person's garden betrays the person. It's true. There is a mind of the person seen in their garden. It comes out in a garden. It is a creation. So you have a garden there.

Then in verse 5 and 15 you have this word "till" or "to dress". You do not have a suggestion of that in Genesis 1. You have it here "to do service" or "to work," something with a purpose to it.

Then in verse 15 is the word "to keep". The Lord says, "put him in the garden to till (or to cultivate) and to keep it." The word "to keep" is "to observe" or "to take heed." That is a most remarkable word. Many people have said, "Wasn't it wrong of the Lord to put Adam and Eve into the garden all innocently and just leave them to the wiles of the serpent? How wicked! We would not do that with our children. We would not put them in the very presence of some vile, ferocious, evil thing and leave them to it just to test whether they would be obedient to father or not." People have said that again and again. But here the Lord put the man in the Garden of Eden to cultivate it and to keep it. Keep does not mean to cultivate; it means to take heed, to watch it. The word is "to guard." He was to guard, he was to watch, he was to observe. There is the possible suggestion of a warning, not only over the tree of the knowledge of good and evil, but of the possibility of evil things coming into the garden and deceiving. He was told to guard that garden, to take heed.

In verse 18, 19 and 20 there is another interesting thing. It says simply, "There was not a help meet for him." It says, "I will make him a help meet for him." Then in verse 20 it says, "But there was not found a help meet for him." The word "meet" is literally "as before him." There was not a help as before him. But the word really means simply, "there was not a help answering to him." There again you have something of a purpose. You see God's whole plan was a complement to Adam—something that answered wholly, fully to him, like him, answering to him. It was not him, identically, but answering to him, something original, something responsible, and yet something answering to him, vitally of him, bound up with him, and therefore belonging to each other. That is very, very wonderful as well.

Thus you have here something, in many ways, in the very vocabulary of Genesis 2 which suggests this whole question of destiny or purpose.

Man as He was Created

Now let's look at the chapter itself, and I am going to follow the order of the chapter. Many people do not. They just chop it around, but we will simply follow through the chapter. The first thing you will find in this chapter is man as he was created. This is of tremendous importance: man as he was created (Genesis 2:5–7). Firstly, let's look at his actual creation in verse 7. "The Lord God formed man of the dust of the ground and breathed into his nostrils the breath of life and man became a living soul."

Now, underline these things. The Lord God "formed" and "breathed into" and "man became." This is very important. We find out straightway that there was no evolution over man. Man was the production of God's hand. But he was more than the mere production of God's hand. Whilst we can say that the rest of creation was brought into being by the Word of God, possibly in a rather distant way, with man, God actually fashioned him. He actually created him. He produced him. Man was the very work of His own hands. That immediately sets forth the intimate relationship between man and his Creator. It says, "The Lord God formed man and breathed into him …" You and I were not originally just the creation of God's hand; we have something of God committed to us. God did something. Here it is spoken of like this, "He breathed into his nostrils the breath of life," and man became something.

Now look very carefully. First of all, we have the formation of something, the fashioning of something. Then we have something given of God, deposited by God in that being. Then, as a result of whatever was committed or given, man became something. Something else happened. In other words, firstly, God formed a body. Then He gave something of Himself, imparted something of Himself, and then the body, along with what God imparted, produced something else. So you see straightway, there is a three-fold work here. There is a body, produced by God's hands, something imparted of God, not created, but imparted, and then something created out of the two. Man became. The Lord God formed ... The Lord God breathed into ... Man became ...

The Constitution of Man—the Body

Let's look at it now from this standpoint, from the question of man's constitution. The first thing you note about this is: the dust of the ground. You and I have been made of the dust of the ground. Remember the Lord said to us, "Dust thou art, and unto dust shalt thou return." We were made, our bodies were made from the very dust of the ground and the word *ground* is very interesting. It is the word *adamah*, from which we get the word *Adam*. It is a word used throughout Scripture, of arable soil, or topsoil. It is the red soil, red earth. It is sort of a reddish colour and has got that meaning of a soil or mould of reddish colour. So, first of all, man's body was made out of the dust of the ground.

Now, note another very interesting thing. It distinctly mentions water. Verses 5 and 6 underline the fact that there was something to do with water. It had not rained, it says, and furthermore it talks of the mists. So we find that man's body is evidently a combination of water and the dust of the ground. I think you will find this rather interesting. This is rather technical and I wasn't going to read it but I thought you may find it rather interesting.

Science has found by chemical analysis of the body of man, that its substance is composed of the very same elements as the soil which forms the crust of the earth and the limestone that lies embedded underneath. They are simply carbon, chlorine, phosphorus, fluorine, nitrogen, magnesium, silicon, aluminium, potassium, sodium, calcium, iron, manganese, titanium, oxygen, hydrogen. Some of these appear in very small and minute proportions, but all are within the human body. Carbon, nitrogen, oxygen, hydrogen, constitute for the most part, the soft tissues and fluids of man's body. While bones, or harder parts consist of calcium, the phosphate and carbonate of lime.

Straightway, you have, in a rather remarkable way, the very fact that man's body was made from the dust of the ground, as though God had formed it out of the soil. It has the very elements of the soil in it. You also know that this body of ours is nearly all water. The element of water is very large in it. It is most remarkable. So here, right in Genesis 2, you have firstly our bodies, formed out of the dust of the ground. It evidently had a reddish colour and, as far as we can make out, this human body originally had a certain colour about it. It probably wasn't terribly deep or distinct, but it was there. That's the body.

The Constitution of Man—the Spirit

Now, the second thing you note in verse 7 is: "the breath of life." The Lord God formed man of the dust of the ground and breathed into his nostrils the breath of life. Here again, although we cannot press this too far, the Hebrew is plural, what we call the plural of excellence. It literally is the breath of lives in the plural. This word "life" here is hardly ever used in the singular, so you cannot press it too far. Nevertheless, it is interesting that God's breath into man did produce two kinds of life. The first was the spiritual life and the other is what we call a soulish life or sensual life. Man became a living soul. Something was imparted and something became as a result of what was imparted. That is very, very interesting because it immediately gets us to this fundamental point that man is a spiritual creature.

Man is not just a body and he is not like the rest of creation. The rest of creation are living souls, as we shall see in a moment. Man's living soul has come in a quite unique and special way. We are told about the other living creatures, the other things that have life within them, or soul within them, and whilst the same word is used, it is quite obvious from Genesis 2 that man's soul is different to the soul of an animal. An animal has a soul, but it is not the same as the soul of a human being because man's soul has come into being because of his spirit. God breathed into him and man became a living soul. His soul is the production of God breathing into him.

It is very important that we should understand man's constitution. First, he has a body made of the dust of the ground and water. He then has what we call the breath of life. It is interesting, that in the Word of God, the Word always refers to God as the Father of our spirit and the Creator of our soul. He never calls Himself the Father of our souls. If you look through Scripture, you will never find that phrase: "the Father of our soul". He is always the Father of our spirit; He is the Creator of our soul. So, man, by this breath of life, was constituted a spiritual creature. That is, there was breathed into him something which could answer to God. Just like woman was made to answer to man, God breathed into man something alone which could answer to God, which could correspond to God, which was according to God, which could be the complement of God. Without that spirit, man would always be a mere servile creation. But because God imparted something, man became a being that could answer to God, that whilst being original and responsible, could walk in fellowship with God, in a way which could satisfy God. That is very, very, very important to understand. Man, therefore, has not only a body, he has a spirit.

The Constitution of Man—the Soul

There is another thing about verse 7: "And man became a living soul." If you look through elsewhere, you will find that this word is used of other creatures, yet, here it is quite obviously unique. This amazing thing that we call a soul is somehow the production of the spirit and the body. The spirit and the flesh are always at war. They belong to different realms. They belong to different spheres. God's thought was that there should be something like a mediator between the two. That mediator is the soul, the medium, the thing in between, which could, somehow, translate things from the spirit through the soul to the flesh. At the same time, God could translate things from the flesh to the spirit. So, of course, you cannot see my spirit. You can see my body, you can feel my soul, and, yet, the most essential part of my being is my spirit.

Now, it is in the soul that Satan has done his work. He has cut that spirit off and caused it to cease its function, and has so perverted and distorted that soul beyond all recognition that it has become the battleground of our lives. It is our soul where we feel things. That is where we feel so awful, where we are all the time aggressive, where we are wanting this and wanting that. That is where we have the battle. The battle is on between our soul and the Lord Himself.

It is the most remarkable thing, this trinity. Mind you, you cannot take it too far, but it is amazing how deep this trinity is; it goes through almost everything. It almost seems to be a principle in everything. You have it again in the whole of natural creation, man and God. God's whole thought was that man should be the medium between Him and the creation, the creation and Him. Man was to be the meeting place with God, where God met the creation and where the creation met God. In our little being, we have the same. We have a body, we have a soul, and we have a spirit. The soul is the thing that, as it were, is in between. We need to see that quite clearly. God's whole thought was that we have our constitution of the body, the spirit, which is the absolute primary thing, and the soul, which is, as it were, between the two.

The Conditional Destiny of Man

We have looked at the creation of man, and we have looked at his constitution. Now let us look at what I would describe as his conditional destiny. I could not find another word, somehow, to express what I mean. Man had a conditional destiny. This is very, very important for us to understand. Man, as created, was not holy, was not perfect, was not sinful, and was not evil. He was innocent and that is a very important thing for us to understand.

We somehow think that Adam was perfect, was holy. He was not holy. Adam had the absence of anything. He was created and he was innocent; he had not yet been tested. God's whole thought was that man's destiny lay on a condition. The condition was what we call here in Genesis 2, the tree of life and marriage; what those two things set forth. That was the condition. If man would come by the tree of life into all God's thought over this question of marriage, his destiny was assured. In fact, he had a *limitless* destiny, if only he would come by the one condition that God laid down. In fact, God never put down that as a condition, He gave the condition in the negative. He said, You are not to eat of that thing, not to take that road, not to become that kind of person. So you do see, that when man was first created, he was not holy, he was not perfect, he was not sinful, he was not evil; he was innocent. His whole destiny was literally hinged on the question of whether he came into what the tree of life stood for and what marriage stood for.

The Capacity of Man

The other thing I want you to notice about these two verses is man's capacity, as created in God's original thought of man. The capacity of man was to be indwelt by an infinite God. That is the most marvellous thing in the whole of creation! Only God could conceive of a finite, human creature that could contain the infinite. Only God could conceive of a vessel inside which He, Himself could actually be. It is unbelievable! Our minds reel at that. This is what it means to be a Christian, of course. We have the infinite in the finite. We have the omnipotent in the weak. We have *the* God who created all things and purposes all things, the utterly sovereign and immutable God in here, in this body formed out of the dust of the ground. That is the capacity of man, a capacity to be God-indwelt and God-possessed. That is a tremendous capacity.

Of course, the tree of life is something individual, marriage is something corporate. But there you have the secret. By way of the tree of life, man was to come into utter dependence upon God. That was the kind of life God intended him to live. He was to find the very ability of his life in God's life. He was to find the very meaning of his existence in the life of God. He was to realise his destiny by the life of God, by eating, as it were, the tree of life, being incorporated into God's life. But then, far more wonderful, the infinite God can only fill our little finite vessels, can only fill them like little thimbles. He needs the whole, many of us of His body, knit together, fused into one, to be able to contain an infinite God. That is there in Genesis 2–man's capacity.

You see then, that man was never made an anti-social creature. The principle of man's very creation is corporate. This whole anti-social love of loneliness, this perversion comes from the old man. There is a right kind of loneliness, of course, and it is the kind of loneliness that God develops. It is a loneliness that finds its fullest expression when we are the most limited. Right in the midst of things that are wholly bound together, we have that sense of just being shut up to God alone on issues. We just cannot run to everything and everyone when we know we are shut up to God. We are alone, yet, we are absolutely part of each other. It is altogether different than this other kind of loneliness that is an anti-social thing, a perverted thing, an embittering thing, a sour thing; that kind of poisonous thing. So you see, you have man's capacity to be indwelt by God. That was our original capacity as created by God.

Then, even perhaps just as wonderful, our capacity was to be able to represent God. Now, that is a remarkable thing, but it says quite clearly in the Word: "God is the head of Christ; Christ is the head of man, and man is the head of the woman. There is a sensing in which we are ambassadors for Christ. We represent God. We are God's vice-regents, the whole thought of our being in His image and after His likeness, is representative. The whole question of authority and dominion and service is linked with being the representative of God. It is being like God, our likeness to God, our being conformed to His image, which is the measure in which we can exercise any authority or really serve the Lord. You cannot just do this and do that, hop into a college, go for a few months, and then go out to the field and think you are serving the Lord. That is not the way. The whole question of service is linked with how much we are like the Lord and what the Lord is really conforming us to be. Out of that comes our authority and our service.

Then, note too that God gave man a capacity for infinite increase of knowledge. You have no idea of the capacity of the spirit within you and within me. You see, that spirit is not a creation. That spirit is an impartation. It is something which God is able, as it were, to expand, and to expand, and to expand. You have got all of eternity to just go on learning. You see, you have a capacity for it. You have a capacity to absorb, to understand. I am not saying we will ever become as infinite as God Himself. That is the whole point of the body. We just cannot, we are not made like that, but we have a capacity for infinite knowledge, a knowledge which knows no end.

4.
Man's Choice

It is hard to go back over what we have said previously, except simply to remind you that the key to the difference between Genesis chapter 1 and chapter 2 is that chapter 1 is the fact of creation and chapter 2 is the purpose of creation. That is the key to those two chapters. For instance, if an order is given, Genesis chapter 1 is the historical order of creation; it gives us something of the order, the way things came. If there is any clue at all in these opening chapters as to method, then it is in Genesis 1. Genesis 2, as you remember we found out last time, is quite different from Genesis 1. The whole vocabulary used, and indeed, even the words used suggest purpose and destiny. The very words used in this chapter, give us a clue as to its meaning.

You will note another thing about chapter 2, which mentioned last time. Genesis 2 is, in a very real way, figurative. Though not wholly figurative, neither is it wholly literal. It is a chapter which has much within it of symbols, something of the oriental imagery of the word. We cannot go back over how we explained this last time; nevertheless, we have to understand this, if we are going to understand why Genesis 2 is so different. For you see, Genesis 2 gives a completely different order than Genesis 1. It tells us that man was the beginning. Genesis 1 tells us that man was the apex, the climax, or the consummation, the crown, if you like, of creation. It just tells us this happened, that happened, the next happened, the other happened, and last of all, God created man. He was the crown of it all. He was the top stone. But Genesis 2 says God first formed man out of the dust of the ground, then everything else came into being. He planted the garden and the trees, He caused the trees to grow up, and then He caused the animals and the birds to come forth. In Genesis 2 we find that man is the centre of everything. He is the reason for everything. He is the heart of it. Genesis 2 begins with man. Genesis 1 ends with man. In Genesis 1, man is the crown of it all, the consummation of God's work. In Genesis 2, man is the beginning of God's work. Now, the difference is simple. The first is historical order and method. The second is the purpose. Everything was created because of man. Man lies at the heart of it all. That is very important for us to understand. Genesis 2 sets forth something of the purpose of God.

Another thing that has been of great concern to me about these first three chapters of Genesis is that we should never, ever again, even subconsciously, come to these chapters with the kind of mentality: "Oh, this is child's play. The first three chapters of Genesis, oh, that is the shallows. That is all very, very simple." Many of us subconsciously, having been brought up in schools that now do not teach the Word of God as it should be taught, have got this mentality that, "Well, there has been so much controversy over the first few chapters of Genesis, so much conflict that, really, you are walking on very unsafe ground when you are treading on these chapters.

The Fundamental Nature of the First Three Chapters of Genesis

However, it is my own firm conviction that the first three chapters of the Bible are absolutely fundamental to the whole of Scripture. If we, for any reason at all, dismiss anything of these first three chapters, we must, of necessity, be in error in all the rest that we believe. You cannot dismiss the first three chapters of Genesis and walk in truth. It is an impossibility, and hence I believe we have the conflict because the enemy knows it. There is the sense in which the whole of the Bible is telescoped into these three chapters. For instance, here in Genesis 2 you have everything, everything in the Bible, in seed form. Genesis chapter 3 would be without real meaning if it was not for this second chapter of Genesis. The importance then, of this chapter, is tremendous. As I said last

... here in Genesis 2 you have everything, everything in the Bible, in seed form

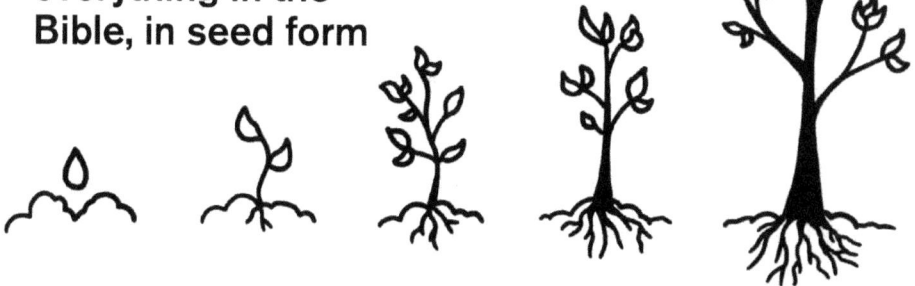

time, and I do feel I ought to reiterate this: if we could only see what the Holy Spirit has written in the second chapter of Genesis, it would deliver us from a tremendous amount of difficulty in our Christian lives.

Evangelical Christianity does not touch the difficulties. That is the trouble. It only scratches the circumference. It tells people to make a decision. It brings them to the Lord. It tells them their work is witnessing and service and then they are left there. Genesis 2 gets right down to the basic difficulties, and this whole deceiving work of the enemy, which, of course, we have to remember when we come to the Lord; we are not just wholly delivered from it. We have got our old nature, and that old nature is just as deceived as ever, and I'm afraid is as ready to make an alliance with the enemy as ever it was. There is ground there, and that is one of the great needs for us to understand. What was God's purpose in man? How did He constitute man originally? What was really man's destiny? If we get those things clear, then when we come to Genesis 3 and find out what has happened to man, we will have a picture of the whole thing. We can really understand something more of the real meaning that is within our salvation.

I do not believe we can understand our salvation in any full way, in any effective way, until we have understood something of Genesis 2 in practice. If we don't understand Genesis 2, we just don't know from what we are saved, we don't know why we really need to be saved, we don't know into what we are saved, and we don't understand the end of our salvation. Our salvation, after all, is only God's undoing of the work of Satan, and starting all over again, renewing us in the image of His own Son. Here you have it in this chapter.

I want you to see that in Genesis 2 you have man in his relationship to everything else. Man is the centre of the whole creation of God. What was God's thought in man? God's thought in man was that man should be the link between God Himself and the creation. In other words, there was something about man which made him the crown of the natural creation. He was the apex of the natural creation, but there was also something about man which made him essentially part of God, and therefore, God and creation meet in man. Do you understand that? In Genesis chapter 1, man is the crown of the natural creation. He is the highest thing in the natural creation, the most wonderful thing, the most unique part of the natural creation, the most intelligent, if you want to put it that way, in the whole natural creation. But in Genesis 2, we find that man was not made a super-animal. He was not made just a natural being much more wonderful than all other creatures. We find in Genesis 2 that man was made for God and was, as it were, to be the most amazing vehicle, or vessel, in which God Himself should live. That is the most amazing thing of all! God has made the natural creation. In that, He has put man, and man was to be the thing in which God lived! Not just in one man but in the whole race! We shall see that as we continue.

The Creation of Man

There are four things that we find in Genesis 2:5–7 as we noted last time. We looked at the creation of man, then we looked at his constitution, then we noticed that he had a conditional destiny, and lastly we noticed his capacity. Simply, what is man's creation? God formed man of the dust of the ground and breathed into him the breath of life, and man became a living soul. Therefore, we know straightway that man is a direct and personal creation of God. God formed man in a distinct and personal way. There was something unique about the creation of man. God formed him. Then have you noticed the words "God formed," which is "to fashion" or "constitute," that is the word used there. He formed man, He breathed into him the breath of life; that is, God did not only create something, He imparted something!

Man is not just a creation of God; God is the Father of our spirits. He is the Father of spirits, Father of lives. That is, He imparted something. That is why Adam is called a "son of God." By Luke, he is called the son of God in the sense that God imparted something of Himself. He breathed into him the breath of life. Then man became a living soul. The imparting of something of God into man brought into being this third part of man, the intermediate part of man, which we call the soul. He became a living soul. It is the word that is used elsewhere in scripture for souls of animals, but here it is used in a quite unique way, obviously because of the method by which man's soul was produced.

The Constitution of Man

You know, of course, man's constitution—man is spirit, soul, and body. He is, first of all, dust of the ground, the word used is *adamah* which is red earth, or topsoil. Water and soil are the constituents in man's body. Then secondly, man had the breath of life breathed into him by God. The Hebrew is plural: "breath of lives." The plural of excellence–cannot take it too far as to mean some kind of life, really, although some people would like to think that it means two kinds of lives, the breath of lives, spiritual life and soulish life. Certainly, it does mean a certain kind of life, unique life, it is a plural which denotes something excellent, something superlative, something that has to be emphasised and underlined. God breathed a certain kind of life into man. He gave His own life, something of Himself He imparted to man, and then man also has a living soul, a soul which is his personality, which is also part of him. His spirit corresponds to God.

The Conditional Destiny of Man

Then you also note that he has a conditional destiny. Man's destiny was not an automatic thing. He had a conditional destiny. He was not perfect. He was not, in that sense, holy. He was not evil. He was not sinful. Man was innocent, but man was warned. He was innocent, but he was warned. God had warned him very clearly of the danger of taking a certain line, choosing a certain type of life and he was left the choice. In verse 15, Adam was put into the garden to dress or till, and to guard or keep it. The word is "to observe," "to watch over" it. We believe there is a possibility there, an implication that God warned Adam about some invisible antagonist in the atmosphere that Adam had to watch. He had to take heed. There was something which was not for God but was against God. Adam's whole destiny was absolutely focused upon what we call the tree of life in the midst of the garden, and the whole meaning of marriage; what marriage really means, spiritually. Upon those two things, Adam's destiny, man's destiny, was conditioned.

The Capacity of Man

Beyond that, of course, man has a capacity; well, that is a really wonderful thing, the capacity of man. He is the only creature in creation that answers to God because he has a spirit, which is the same essential character as God, and, therefore, man has a capacity. Man is capable of being indwelt by God. Indwelt by God personally, that is the capacity of man, and you know, we have grown used to it, we hear it so often, we read about it in the Bible, we sing about it, we pray about it, we talk about it, and we have all grown awfully used to it. It no longer leaves us overwhelmed. But when we sit back and think a bit—if we could, in a virgin way, in a new way—what a wonderful thing that is just to sit back and let it sink in! You and I have a capacity which is unique, a capacity for God! We can be indwelt by God. We can be possessed by God. We can represent God. We are the only creatures on the whole earth that can actually represent God! We can be the image of God. We should be the image of God in this creation, representing Him, expressing Him. What a capacity!

The most wonderful thing to me is the capacity for an ever-growing knowledge of God. "What we shall be," John says. For we know if we are now sons of God, we don't know what we shall be. If we are children of God now, what is it going to be one day, in the ages of the ages? It is just going to be an eternal unfolding of vistas, which would do us no good to see at present, otherwise, we would all be lost in the wonder of it. However, heaven is not going to be as some people think, you know, just sort of looking through binoculars at one particular spot. Many people have that subconscious idea that they will all be around the throne, looking through the vast crowds, down the arena, upon the throne there— that sort of thing. Oh no! Heaven is going to be a most amazing realm, a most amazing life. You see, we have a capacity. We have a capacity at present to get to know God. We are getting to know the Lord perhaps through a difficult way down here, but when we are freed from sin and freed from our fallen nature, then we should be let loose into a capacity for God which is capable of increase, of enlargement. God is inexhaustible. He is unsearchable. He will always be thinking up something new into which to lead His children and to uncover to His children. There is something very, very wonderful about man.

I hope that makes you realise what a wonderful creature, in a modest and humble way, man was as God created him. What a wonderful creature! There is something wonderful about man. We marvel at the natural creation, but I believe God marvels at man much more. Man is God's most wonderful creation in every way. His body is wonderful! And what a wonderful thing a soul is! Who knows the soul of a man? Even now, we have these men called psychologists, psychiatrists, who just go around in giddy circles because they have not yet really come to a real understanding of the capacity of the soul. Oh, the amazing capacity of the human soul!

But you know, we, as the Lord's people, are discovering something of the capacity of the spirit, and that is the most wonderful realm of all! Because that is the realm which is limitless; the other has its defined restrictions and limits, but you see, the spirit can swim in God. There are no boundaries to God, and the spirit is that part of man which can be lost in God eternally, and never reach the end. It can never get to the boundaries of God (if there are any) or discover everything there is to know about Him. It will just never happen! The amazing thing is, you see, that the spirit is something which can be lost in God for all eternity. That is the wonder of it!

So you see something of man as he was created.

Man's Probation

I want to speak now about man on probation (Genesis 2:8–17). I think it almost goes without saying, and we shall see this more as we go on through this chapter, that God's creation of man, God's whole thought in the creation of man, was to have someone that could respond to Him, and that could answer to Him, who was capable of (oh, our human terms just fail here) receiving God, of holding God, and of walking with God.

That immediately brings up the whole question of man's will, a subject in which I am not going to get lost this evening. (I would probably give you a lot more problems than I solve.) The whole point is simply that when God created man, the one thing He was clear on, was that He would not have an automatic and impersonal machine. The whole Word of God bears that out. God's thought in creation was not a creature that had to do certain things if you pressed certain buttons, but a creature that could and would. In other words, you have it all very beautifully portrayed later on in this whole question of marriage. The Lord is not going to be satisfied by people who have to come to Him, and for whom He has sort of pressed certain buttons so that they come. That would not satisfy God. God is going to have someone who is there because she loves Him. She is going to stay there because she loves Him. That is, of course, the cause of many of our unfortunate ideas about being with the Lord. Some of us, I'm afraid, are only with the Lord because of duty. Oh, no, no, the Lord will get us through on all that, even if it takes a big battering, He will get us through to the place where we are there because we love Him, and we will stay there because we love Him.

Well, that is the whole purpose here. God did not want something automatic and He did not want something impersonal. He wanted a man, a race, a creation that would willingly open its arms to God, and say, "I want to go this way." God could define two types of man. One, which was intimately bound up with Himself, and the other, which was intimately bound up with man himself. He could know that man would say, "I want Thee. I will be with Thee. I will take this course. I will be wholly given up to Thee."

There is a tremendous amount bound up in that because, of course, man was so creative, and so constituted that, in the thought of God, man was only constituted for one of those types. God's whole thought was that man was so constituted that he could not be happy in any other realm but the realm that God had prepared. Nevertheless, God gave him the choice: would you go, would you come and live in the realm for which you have been constituted? for which I have created you? or would you prefer to have everything in yourself, and be the master of your own destiny? choose everything for yourself?

You know how I feel about these things, the question of election and the question of free will, and the way the two tie up together. However, what we see, and it is quite clear here, is that man is on probation. God wanted man to be with Him because man *wanted* to be with Him. He was going to possess man because man wanted to be possessed. He was going to dwell in man because man wanted to be dwelt in. He was going to open His heart to man because man wanted God to open His heart. That was the line the Lord was going to take. There is no doubt about it. If He had wanted to, He could have made something quite different that would have had to, but no, that was not the line the Lord took.

The Two Trees

So we come to the significance of the tree of life and the tree of the knowledge of good and evil. Note that one is in the midst of the garden and the other is not mentioned as to where it was. It may have been in some corner of the garden for all we know, but the tree of life was in the midst of the garden. Now, what do these trees stand for? We know, of course, that the tree of life speaks supremely of the Lord Jesus. We see through scripture that He is, in a very real way, the tree of life–the life of God. But trees in scripture do often speak of man. (It is remarkable if you look through scripture and discover it). Trees are often a symbol of man. For instance, in Psalm 1, the psalmist speaks of us being like a tree planted beside the river whose leaves shall not fade. In another place, Jeremiah speaks of us either being a little dwarf juniper or being a cedar. In many other places, man is spoken of in these terms—an upright man is likened to a palm tree. The cedars of Lebanon are often a figure of dignity. The acacia wood of the tabernacle, for instance, always speaks of the humanity of the Lord Jesus. We could go through many Scriptures which speaks of trees, or wood symbolising humanity.

It is my own conviction here that the tree of life and the tree of the knowledge of good and of evil represent two types of men. Now, forgive me if you have heard this, but I am going to say it again because we are dealing with it here and it needs to be said. The tree of life speaks, first of all, of a God-centred, God-conscious, and God-dependent man. That is, a man who is centred in God by the life of God. He is dependent upon God because he lives by God's life. He is conscious of God because he is possessed and owned by the life of God. He is a man who has received the life of God, and has become a dependent being, a God-dependent being. He is not independent, not self-dependent, but God-dependent. God is at the heart of his being, and the man is centred and focused in God. That man, to live, is dependent on God. That, to me, is the tree of life. Look at the Lord Jesus. The Lord Jesus is and speaks of the tree of life. Have you ever found a more God-dependent, God-centred, and God-conscious man than the Lord Jesus? You will not find one! The Lord Jesus was absolutely and wholly that.

On the other side, you have got the tree of the knowledge of good and evil. What did Satan say about this? He said that if you take and eat of this tree you will be as God; you will be equal with God. You will have this something inside of you by which you will be able to make your own decisions. You will be able to determine yourself what is right. The knowledge will be in your *self*. That is the knowledge of good and evil. And the tree of the knowledge of good and evil stands always to me for a *self*-conscious, *self*-centred, and *self*-dependent life, as opposed to the other.

So today in the world, you see straightway, you have two types of humanity, and they are totally different. Their constitution is basically and totally different. You have on the one side a *God*-conscious, *God*-centred, and *God*-dependent humanity, which is in Christ, and on the other side you have a *self*-centred, *self*-conscious, and *self*-dependent humanity, which is in Adam. That was the choice. Everything, everything hung upon Adam's choice. Would he choose the tree of life, which was so prominently placed in the very centre, or the heart of the garden, or would he find out about the other and take that? That was the choice for man. Man had been so created, so constituted that he was made for the tree of life. Made for it! If he took the other course, he would become a pervert. I hope that does not shock you, but we were all born perverts. There is something utterly perverted about us, and, of course, that simple fact is written in our experience from our births. We grow up with it, all the time, all through life, we are conscious of something perverted. Oh, if you give man all the money, all the popularity, and everything that he desires, he still knows, deep down, there is something he doesn't have and he does not know what it is. All the time there is something in him that tells him: this isn't it, this isn't it, this isn't it. It can be satiated for the moment, but it is still not it. It goes on. You see, there is something there quite deep, deep down in man.

The tree of life, of course, was fulfilled in our Lord Jesus. He is the fulfilment of the tree of life. He is the tree of life in that sense. He brought in a new kind of humanity, didn't he? When He came, He was transfigured upon that mount of transfiguration. God's seal was upon that kind of humanity. Then, when He went to the cross, He finalised everything of the last Adam. He took everything about us naturally into Himself and died! That was the end of a race! When He was raised again on the third day, He was the head of a new creation, head of the new man. He brought in a new kind of humanity. When He was raised, one of the first things He did was to breathe into them and say: "Receive the Holy Spirit." Why did He do that? Because He wanted to impress upon them the beginning of a new creation, God was breathing into them. So you see something of the wonder of all this.

God's Delight

Then you will notice the other amazing thing about this garden. Have you noticed that everything to do with the garden is life? Everything to do with this garden is life—mark the arrangement. First of all, you have the tree of life in the midst of the garden. Then, out from the garden, you have a river flowing, and this river branches into four great rivers that water the earth. From the book of Revelation and from Ezekiel, we understand that the tree of life was almost at the source of the river. It was in the midst of the river almost. It was on one side of the river and on the other. What does this mean? First of all, you have got a garden called the garden of Eden, which means "delight." The delight of God. So you have a clearly defined boundary and it is called delight. It is both the delight of God and it was meant to be the delight of man. In this clearly defined boundary, clearly defined garden, the whole delight of God was centred, and the whole delight of man would come to its fulfilment. Man would be satisfied, as it were, within the boundaries of this garden.

I have said that Genesis 2, in many ways, has symbolism about it, and I am quite sure that Eden is one of the symbols. I am not saying that there was not a little garden, but I am quite clear from the way that the Holy Spirit takes it through the Bible, that Eden is a symbol. He speaks of Satan being there in the garden of Eden. He speaks elsewhere of Eden. What does Eden mean? Eden tells us that God's delight can only rest in certain things. His delight is bounded. His delight is to do with the tree of life at the heart and a river that waters everything. It is fourfold. It is universal and goes to the four corners of the earth almost. We will never be able to find out where this river went. We have understood that the flood has changed the face of the East, and, therefore, we do not know quite where two of the rivers would have gone. Great suggestions have been made. Calvin thought it was the Ganges River and others thought it was other great rivers. However, one thing we do know is, symbolically, it speaks of a mighty river of life that is going out and giving life and fertility to the whole earth. From where does it come? It comes from this garden. It comes, at the heart of it, from the tree. The tree is on either side of the river.

Now, the tree speaks of the character and type of life; the river, always in scripture, speaks of service and ministry. It is something that is life giving. The tree is the type. It is a character. God says have this type of life. Have this character and then we can get on with the job and there is ministry that can flow out.

You will note, of course, that you have the same things at the end of the Bible. Instead of Adam, a fallen creation, you have a city. From within the city, there flows out a river that waters the whole earth. On either side of the banks of the river there is the tree of life bearing its fruit. What does this all mean? It means, first of all, God's delight is in her. That is, the city is God's delight. It is there that God can be pleased. It is there that God can be satisfied, and nowhere else. God's satisfaction is there. Why is it there? It is because there is a certain character there, and because of the certain character, there is a certain ministry. Everything is exactly as God would have it. At the end, you have a ministry that is flowing out to the ends of the earth because God has a certain kind of man in the glory with Himself. God has a vessel, and there is God filling the vessel, possessing the vessel, expressing Himself through the vessel. So, in the end, we have this wonderful, three-fold symbol: the city, the tree, and the river. At the beginning, we have the garden, the tree, and the river. At the beginning it is man's probation. At the end, it is the securing of God's work. God has it in the end.

Here in Genesis, you have only the man on probation. The choice is set before man. (I am going to put it now in this way as if we are going back to kindergarten.) It is as if God said, "Now, look here, Adam. Here is a garden. See it? It has clearly defined boundaries. Adam, I am going to call this garden *My delight*. There is nothing else that can really satisfy Me. I can say that it is good. I can stand back and say that I see it all, and it is good. But to be delighted, to be satisfied, to rest, Adam, is this garden. In the midst of the garden, Adam, there is a tree and, Adam, this tree stands for a certain kind of man—a man that lives in Me and I live in him. That is the kind of man. He is centred in me and dependent on Me for everything. He has chosen that life. Because of that, Adam, I can use him to bring life to the ends of the earth".

Well, that is the simplest way possible I can explain something of Adam's probation. Man was made for service in that sense, and the river stands for that ministry and service—life-giving, life-creating service. But it all comes and stems from the kind of man that God wants. If he is the kind of man the tree of life depicts, then the river flows out! You notice, of course, how beautifully it is put. In verse 9, it says clearly that the tree of life was in the midst of the garden, and the tree of the knowledge of good and evil. Then verse 10 says: "And a river went out of Eden to water the garden; and from thence it was parted and became four heads," or four rivers. Then it tells about the four rivers and where they flowed to, and so on. The whole of this little portion is taken up with the Garden of Eden. There is another interesting thing. It is only in these verses, Genesis 2:8–17, that the Garden of Eden is mentioned. It is only mentioned once more in Genesis 3. It is very interesting. The Garden of Eden is mentioned three times there, and the tree of life and the tree of the knowledge of good and evil are mentioned only here in this chapter, in these few verses. It is all to do with Adam's probation! It has everything to do with Adam's probation here.

The Enemy's Deceiving Work

I will just say one more thing about the delight of God. You and I have been made for God. The enemy's deceiving work is all the time to tell us that if we centre everything on God, and if we give ourselves wholly for God's possession, we shall be miserable people, that the way of delight lies in self-fulfilment, whatever that means, whether it be in another person, or whether it be in ourselves. That is the way that the enemy always speaks to us. Of course, it is the same battle all over again! It is only the same old battle: the tree of life and the tree of the knowledge of good and evil. "Come," says the enemy, "You fool. Do you think that the way of your delight lies along that line? Do you think, you poor creature, that God can satisfy you? You have a body. You have a soul. You can only be satisfied by earthly things, by natural things. Do you honestly think that God can satisfy you? Do you think that you can be delighted by God? Oh, no! God may need you for *His* delight, but *you* will not find delight by going after Him!"

So the enemy goes on, and so we all still fall to the enemy's tactics; they haven't changed over the years. He comes along the same ground of self-conscious life. He just makes us feel. He rouses our self-consciousness, our self-centredness, our (we like to call it) independence, our self-dependence, you see? He gets us along that line saying, "You will be alright!" It is all very well to believe this in theory. It is good in the head. It is a good, nice, clean stuff to believe, but, of course, it does not work out in our experience. We live in an awful world, and you were made like this you see."

The enemy breathes his lies. The thing that we never, never, never, believe is the simple fact that we were created and constituted for God. Whilst these other things can satisfy us for a moment, they cannot satisfy us fully. They cannot! That is the line along which we have to move and prove it. Sometimes the Lord allows us to go a long way along that line in order to prove it. We become miserable, sour, empty people. We cannot understand it. We have what we wanted. We satiated ourselves, our own lives, and we are still not delighted people. Do you see what I mean? No, the way of delight lies along the line of God's delight.

Let me put it another way. The way of satisfaction lies along the way of God's satisfaction. Let me put it in yet another way. The way of rest lies along the way of God's rest. You will never know anything of the garden, and of what a garden in God's Word speaks of: peace, delight, order, joy, fruitfulness, and so on, unless you come to this place. God has delight. When you come within the boundaries of this city, you are in the place of God's delight. In the end, oh, believe me, you will know what it is to be delighted, absolutely delighted. Everything else will fall into its right perspective and place there. But you see, the probation goes on. Even now, we find ourselves in the way of this probation.

Gold, Bdellium, and Onyx Stone

Now, you will note three things which often used to bewilder me: gold, bdellium, and the onyx stone. We often think: why, are these three things mentioned? What are these doing in this second chapter of Genesis? Why does the Holy Spirit underline that the river compasses a land where there is wonderful gold found, bdellium, and the onyx stone? Well, these again are, in certain ways, figurative. They speak of certain things. God says His life has certain conditions, and the conditions of His life are found within these three things: gold, bdellium and the onyx stone.

The first is gold. Gold is all the way through the Word. It is found everywhere through the Word. What does gold speak of? It speaks of many things, but we can cover everything by saying that gold speaks of the divine nature. God has said: This life is inseparably bound up with My nature. This life I cannot commit to anything but My nature. If you choose to have another kind of nature, My life cannot come. My life will not come. Death comes along that line.

You see, if we sow of the flesh we shall, of the flesh, reap corruption. If we sow of the spirit, we shall, of the spirit, reap life everlasting. God can commit Himself to His nature, the divine nature. We are partakers of the divine nature. So you see, God says that first of all, the first thing, the first condition for this man is that he must have the divine nature. Give him the divine nature and God can give him everything.

The second thing you will notice is bdellium. What is bdellium? It is only mentioned in one other place in Scripture, in Numbers 11:7. Oh, the rabbis have written books on it, and the early fathers argued about it, and the Reformers questioned it. Everyone has 'had a go' as it were, about this question of bdellium. What is bdellium? Some rabbis say it is a little pearl found in the Red Sea. Many other rabbis say it is a kind of herb-like myrrh from which we get a kind of incense. However, I think the Scripture itself tells us what bdellium is meant to represent. It is meant to represent heavenly sustenance. Whatever else we do not know about bdellium, it is like manna, and it speaks of being sustained from heaven. Now, whether that is so of bdellium or not, whether that is what its meaning is, it is absolutely true about this kind of life about which we are talking–the life of God. It can only be sustained from heaven. You see, that just shows the kind of life it is. It is a heavenly life, and therefore it has to have a heavenly sustenance. Its growth, its development, its reproduction, its increase, is all along the line of heavenly sustenance.

If you go out and feed yourself upon sensual things and earthly things, you cannot possibly know an increase of spiritual life. Spiritual life needs heavenly sustenance. It needs heavenly food. Really what the Lord was teaching Adam on his probation was: "Adam, the whole point about this tree of life and this river of life is simply that, firstly, you have to have a certain kind of nature, otherwise there can be no life. You cannot have My life. You cannot become the vessel for My life unless you have a certain kind of nature, My nature. Secondly, that nature has to be sustained from heaven. Its development, its growth, its increase, it is all dependent on Me."

God gave the manna. What did manna speak of? Well, there was nothing natural about manna. It was a heaven-given provision and it was a miraculous provision. When you think of a whole host that was fed by manna in the wilderness for something like 40 years, then you realise what a remarkable thing the manna was! You see? God was providing. The provision for this kind of life is heavenly. That means a walk with the Lord, doesn't it?

The other thing you notice about this life is the onyx stone. Now we need to turn to two passages of the Word to get an understanding of the onyx stone.

And thou shalt take two onyx stones, and grave on them the names of the children of Israel: six of their names on the one stone, and the names of the six that remain on the

other stone, according to their birth. With the work of an
engraver in stone, like the engravings of a signet, shalt thou
engrave the two stones, according to the names of the children
of Israel: thou shalt make them to be inclosed in settings of
gold. And thou shalt put the two stones upon the shoulder-
pieces of the ephod, to be stones of memorial for the children
of Israel: and Aaron shall bear their names before Jehovah
upon his two shoulders for a memorial. (Exodus 28:9–12)

You notice that Exodus 28:20 says, "and the fourth row a beryl, and an onyx and a jasper." The onyx stone in the breastplate of the high priest had upon it a name engraved: Asher, the stone of the tribe of Asher.

Now look at Deuteronomy 33:24–25: "And of Asher he said, Blessed be Asher with children; Let him be acceptable unto his brethren, And let him dip his foot in oil. Thy bars shall be iron and brass; And as thy days, so shall thy strength be."

What does the onyx stone speak of? It speaks of dependence on and in God. Do you know where the onyx stone was on the high priest? It was on either shoulder, and it was on his heart. It spoke of a position—a position in Christ before God, which was absolutely dependent upon God's grace. How come you are borne on the shoulders of Christ? How come you are in the heart of Christ? It is but by the grace of God.

You are dependent—if you were taken out of position, the Lord help you! If you were to start and say, "I got there myself, I did this, I did that, I did the other, and now I am a child of God," where would you be? You can only come saying, "God took hold of me. God opened my eyes. God brought me to His side, and now He has borne me upon His shoulders and upon His heart, into the very presence of God."

What, therefore, does the onyx stone speak of in relationship to the life of God? Well, it speaks of three very wonderful things. It speaks firstly, of a position which we have mentioned. Secondly, it speaks of an authority. It was like a signet ring, the engraving on the signet. It speaks of authority. You know when we speak of the Lord Jesus, prayer in the name of Jesus, what was He saying? He was simply saying, I am giving you an authority. But can we just use that authority for anything? Can I get on my knees tonight and say, "Lord, I want a Rolls Royce, please provide it by tomorrow morning? I ask for it in the name of the Lord Jesus," just like that, and expect to get it? No, my authority is dependent upon the Lord, isn't it? This life of God is totally dependent on God. Our position in Christ is dependent on Him. Our authority is dependent on Him. A very wonderful thing that you get in these few verses in Deuteronomy, is that our security, or strength, is dependent upon God. "As thy days are, so shall thy strength be," or thy rest, or thy security.

It speaks here of his foot being dipped in oil, and his shoes being iron and brass. Isn't that wonderful? His foot being dipped in oil—now what does that speak about? What does oil speak about in the Word of God? It speaks of the Holy Spirit. It says, you see, that the whole of this man's livelihood, his pilgrimage, his service—he has to walk—everything to do with his feet is dependent upon the Holy Spirit. It is the Holy Spirit who will shod him in shoes of iron, in shoes of brass, and as long as he lives, God will be his security. That is a very wonderful thing.

To put it in very simple words, the onyx stone means this: God said, this life is firstly dependent on a certain kind of nature in you. Secondly, it is dependent on heavenly sustenance, being sustained by Myself. Thirdly, its whole security and position is dependent on Me. As long as your days are, so shall your security be. In other words, if you have that kind of nature, that divine nature by spiritual birth, and if that new creation in you is being sustained against every antagonistic force in this universe by heavenly sustenance, God says, "I will undertake to keep you, from the beginning to the end. I will see that your shoes are the right kind of shoes. They will not wear out. I will see to that, and, as long as you live, I will be your rest and your security. Now, you see, that is all dependent on the kind of life you lead. That is why some of us live such restless, insecure, weak lives, because we have not got the life! We are depending on another kind of nature. God says, "That brings death. I cannot touch that. I cannot sustain that. I cannot give you food day by day to keep that alive. I have to just allow that to die! But given this kind of nature, and this kind of life, I will sustain it from Heaven and, not only will I sustain it, I will undertake to be its security. I am the Alpha and the Omega, the Beginning and the End— you can't get beyond that—the First and the Last." The Lord comprehends the whole of our existence.

Sometimes we wonder: why did Adam fail? I am sure that Adam had a certain understanding of it. I don't believe that God just said, "Look here, you must do that, lest I do that." I believe that God explained something to him. That gold, and that bdellium, and that onyx were explained. It was there in symbolic form but it was explained to him. Oh, Adam, God was saying, Adam, you take this way, you take this kind of life, you have this kind of nature, and I will undertake to keep you. You don't have to be frightened about Satan, I will sustain you, and I will be your security. But no, Adam went the other way. Well, that is another story.

Man's Destiny

Now, I would just like to say a few more words about the last few verses of this second chapter of Genesis. I want to point out here what I call "man and his destiny". We have had man created, man on probation, now the last part of this chapter (Genesis 2:18–25), speaks of man and his destiny.

Do you remember what I touched upon last time? I said something like this: Is it not feasible to believe that the creation of man was in God's thought to be the beginning of a far, far, far greater thing than a natural creation? It was to be the beginning of a spiritual creation, of which the natural was only the forerunning probation, according to that principle in I Corinthians 15:45–47 where the Lord just says, "Howbeit that is not first which is spiritual, but that which is natural." First the earthly, then the heavenly. I believe that was something in God's mind from the beginning. The natural was going to be but a school. What was this garden? I believe it was going to be a school, a school in the natural creation. Really, the whole goal to God was: "I'm not going to end here. I am not going to end with an Eden. I am going to end with a city coming down from heaven. I am not going to end with an Eden coming out from the earth. I am going to end with a city coming down from heaven!"

Some people think: "Oh, no, no, no, no! That was all a result of the fall. That New Jerusalem, that Bride of the Lamb, that wife of the Lamb, that is all the result of the fall." Oh no, I am not so sure it was the result of the fall. Thank God it has come, even if there has come a fall! By the cross, by the Lord Jesus, we have gotten it back. We are in it. But the wonder to me is that it may well have been God's original thought, that this Eden was the school for a far more wonderful thing, a heavenly thing, a spiritual creation, which was going to come out of man's perfect obedience in the garden. It was going to be his probation. He was going to get through, and then he was going to go on.

The whole point was this: had man got a resurrection body then? I don't know. I am asking you to think about it—was God's thought a resurrection body? Well, you have to go to scripture and look that up and follow that through. Was God's thought that, without possibly even such a thing as death, there should come a certain point in Adam's history, if he went on with the Lord, when there would be a wonderful change? Just like some of us will know if the Lord comes before we die, in the twinkling of an eye, this old body will suddenly become a new body, a resurrection body. But was that going to happen in the garden anyway, without him being laid to rest in the earth? If Adam had gone on with the Lord, and had obeyed, would he have come to the point where God said, "We have gotten through this stage of things. We have gotten through this class in school, now you're going on into a new class". Adam's body would change in the twinkling of an eye, and it would have moved on, being released from that sphere into another sphere–I don't know. I leave it to you to think about it. I say it as speculation and we must be careful of that.

However, there is one thing I am sure about and that was that the garden of Eden was but a forerunning, natural probation, to something far, far more wonderful, far more wonderful. I believe that God was going to bring the Lord Jesus into that garden, even without the fall. His thought was the wife prepared for the Son of God. That would all have come, even without what we know as the fall, and the whole history in between.

I have said something, of course, about the delight of God and the delight of man. I am going to leave that except to say that this whole question of marriage is summed up just in those few words: the delight of God and the delight of man. Meet Him, actually meet Him, be infused in such a way that each is dependent on the other.

5.
"Now the Serpent ..."

Now we come to Genesis chapter 3. Even with all that is revealed in Genesis 1 and 2, I think you will realise that we do not have the practical explanation for what we have today. If we had only the first two chapters of Genesis, we would have discovered, first of all, that the whole creation is the result of the sovereign activity of God. We would also have found out that man is the result of a sovereign creation of God. He created us quite sovereignly, directly, personally; there was something quite direct about man's creation. We would have also discovered that man, in the thought of God, is the apex of creation. That is, he is the top stone of creation, he is the consummation of it all. In a sense, man is the sum of creation. He crowns the work of God and we would have discovered that everything about the creation and about man was very good. God's thought about the whole thing was that it was very good.

From Genesis 2 we would also have discovered that man was the centre and the beginning of God's work, that is, everything was created, insofar as it was related to God's thought concerning man. There was absolutely nothing created that was not, in some way or another, related to God's purpose concerning man. Man was the beginning of it all, and man was the heart of it all. We would also have discovered that God did not want a kind of machine, and we would have discovered that man is a vessel created by God and the only vessel created by God which is capable of holding God. That was God's thought in man. But man was a vessel who was so constituted that he had a capacity for God. God could actually live in man, in a way that He could not live in anything else. Man could respond to God. Man could walk with God. Man could delight God. Man could satisfy God.

We would have found out all of those things from Genesis 1 and 2. We would have found out that God did not want a "press button machine." We would have found out from Genesis 2 that God wanted a man who would enter, quite voluntarily, into all that God wanted or intended for him. He wanted to know that man was there not out of duty, not out of fear, but out of love. Man wanted to be at the side of God. We would also discover that God had a glorious destiny for man, nothing less than marriage, was God's thought for man. Something that Paul calls a mystery, something which is utterly beyond even our wildest dreams. All that we can say, the only way that we can explain it, is by this term: marriage. God's thought, God's destiny for man, was that by coming, by partaking of the tree of life, man should come to his destiny, which was an indissoluble, indivisible union with Himself in His Son. That was God's thought.

If we had only the first two chapters of Genesis, we would have been very, very, very bewildered. We would have said: Wait, is that everything? Is that what God created? Is that how God created? Well, then, why all this? Why the awful, bloody history of man? Why the breakdown? Why the failure? Why the misery? Where did evil come from? Why are things in disharmony? Why is there so much strife? What about the cesspool that this world is? We would have asked these questions and we would have had no answer.

Genesis 1 and Genesis 2 are very, very wonderful and they are very, very necessary. Genesis 2 is absolutely vital for an understanding even of the gospel. The whole Bible springs out of Genesis 2, but Genesis 3 is the practical side of it all—the explanation. We need to have an explanation. It is very necessary that we should have an explanation. Why do we have bodies like we have? Why do we have appetite like we have? Why do we react like we react? Why is there an inherent rebellion in us against God, even when we are children of God? Why is it that we are so made? Why is the current against us and all the rest of it? Well, Genesis 3 is the explanation, and a very practical explanation of the present. Furthermore, Genesis 3 is the practical answer. You know, that is perhaps the most wonderful thing of all that Genesis 3 has within it—the whole seed of the answer. God's answer is there in the third chapter of Genesis. If we had nothing else, we have the answer there written in the third chapter of Genesis. There is a sense in which out of two small phrases in Genesis 3, the whole Bible springs: "The seed of the woman" and "God clothed them with skins." Out of that everything comes. The whole Bible, really in many ways, is but the evidence of that seed and the war between the seed of the woman, the seed of the serpent, and also between those who have come by the way of the death of another, who have found their standing and acceptance before and with God.

The Presence of Satan

So, we come this evening to Genesis 3 and before we have even read the first few words of Genesis 3, we immediately find a new element. We have an element introduced in the first few verses that is not found anywhere else in the first three chapters or at least the first two chapters. We read this: "Now the serpent ..." "Now the serpent." We have a new element—the devil has been introduced. Right at the very beginning of chapter 3, we have the devil himself introduced. So, we get down to things very, very quickly. Here we are, we're dealing with the present. Why did it all happen? What has happened? Where did it all originate? Why is it like this? Why are we like this? In the first words of the first verse we have the answer: "Now the serpent was more subtle than any beast of the field that the Lord God had made." "The serpent ... the serpent."

Now, there has always been a great argument. Was it an actual serpent? Was it a serpent, as we know a serpent today that the devil mastered, controlled, and so used as to bring about the fall? Or, as some believe, was it simply a term that we know is used throughout scripture for the devil himself? Did he come as a minister of light, an angel of light, and a minster of righteousness into the garden? Well, we are not going to stay with that, but I might just say that Genesis 3 is in many ways a carrying on of Genesis 2. If you remember all that we said about oriental imagery concerning Genesis 2, you will understand a good deal more about Genesis 3. There are one or two things in Genesis 3 of course, which are quite obviously symbolical. There are the cherubim, and the flame of a sword which turned every way, to keep the way, and the tree of life. We believe this to be something that stands for something spiritual throughout the whole Word of God. Now we will look at some of these scriptures.

But I fear, lest by any means, as the serpent beguiled Eve in his craftiness, your minds should be corrupted from the simplicity and the purity that is toward Christ … And no marvel; for even Satan fashioneth himself into an angel of light. (II Corinthians 11:3, 14)

And the great dragon was cast down, the old serpent, he that is called the Devil and Satan, the deceiver of the whole world; he was cast down to the earth, and his angels were cast down with him. (Revelation 12:9)

By the way, the word *old* literally means "ancient." Not as we use it, "that old serpent." Subconsciously, I used to think that was what it meant—"that old serpent." However, it means "that ancient serpent," the devil; we might just remember that. It goes back to the beginning.

And he laid hold on the dragon, the old serpent, which is the Devil and Satan, and bound him for a thousand years. (Revelation 20:2)

Now, you see, from those very few scriptures that the devil is quite consistently called, throughout the Bible, the serpent, that old serpent, the devil. In the first two chapters, we have no mention of the devil or of an angelic form. All we have are one or two possible hints. For instance, we are told that the world was chaos and void. Some people believe that is an evidence of some terrible angelic catastrophe. We are told that Adam was put into the Garden of Eden to till it and to guard it. He was to take heed. He was to watch over it. Those are the only hints that we have, really, that there was any person other than God, Adam, and Eve. We have no suggestion, in these first two chapters, of the existence of the devil himself until we come to chapter 3. Then suddenly, the Lord draws aside the curtain and we see that, behind the whole of creation, there lies something far vaster, far bigger. There is some being that, to put it as we would today, has "fallen out" with God, and has led a faction, a division, and it has ended in a complete break with God. We find that this being is being entirely cast out.

Two passages in the Word are very revealing.

How art thou fallen from heaven, O day-star, son of the morning! how art thou cut down to the ground, that didst lay low the nations! (Isaiah 14:12)

We realise that Isaiah was primarily prophesying about Babylon. He began by speaking about Babylon. Then suddenly, Isaiah is carried obviously far beyond men and kings, and says things that really could not be true about a human being. "O day-star, Lucifer, son of the morning," and so on. In Ezekiel 28, there is an even more remarkable prophecy:

> *Son of man, take up a lamentation over the king of Tyre, and say unto him, Thus saith the Lord Jehovah: Thou sealest up the sum, full of wisdom, and perfect in beauty. (Ezekiel 28:12)*

Now, Ezekiel was speaking at the beginning about the king of Tyre and, in his prophecy, he is carried right beyond the king of Tyre to something that lies behind the king of Tyre. You know the Scripture speaks of world rulers of darkness, that which lies behind the king, behind the dictator, behind the government of the nations. Then we learn a very, very amazing thing. We learn simply this— that kind always begets its own kind. Satan can only produce himself. When we realise that, we have come to the heart of the fall. Satan has produced something. When the prophet takes up his lamentation over Babylon, or when he takes up his lamentation over Tyre, he is perfectly right when he gets beyond what is human and sees, behind the human, the satanic. He sees in the king of Tyre, for instance, only the reproduction, in miniature, of what has happened to Satan himself. He saw the same spirit, the same characteristics, the same hallmark; it was all there.

When we come then to this third chapter of Genesis we find straightway that we are in the presence of Satan. There is a malignant adversary. (This has to be said.) Satan has the most violent antagonism and hatred toward Christ and toward man. I do not believe that Satan does not have a hatred toward man. I believe that Satan hates man. He hates man. He only uses man unto an end. There is something vile in the hatred of Satan for man. You have to recognise this: you are in the presence of a hatred, which is ferocious in its power, a hatred and an antagonism toward Christ and then toward man. You find it throughout the whole of Scripture.

The Destructive Purpose of the Devil

Why does Satan come into the garden? What is he trying to do? Why does he take man and utterly pervert him? Why does he then degrade man and bring man down to a bondage to depravity? After thousands and thousands and thousands of years, we have evidence today, in a much greater and more universal way than even at the beginning, of the depravity and the bondage to depravity that there is in man. It was Satan's whole idea behind it. You have it simply in this hatred of Christ. Satan knows he cannot destroy God's Son, but he is out to destroy God's dwelling place. He knows better than we that, from the beginning, God's thought in man was a vessel, a place to dwell, a place capable of being possessed and indwelt by God, a bride for God's Son. Satan is out to utterly eliminate any possibility of that ever taking place. Then, when Satan said, "I will be like the Most High, I will exalt my throne," and so on, he comes down, and his first attempt is to take away God's man. What is God's purpose concerning His Son? What is God's purpose concerning man? Satan says, "I will take the place of God's Christ. I will take man for myself. I will bring man into a union with myself. I will bring man to myself!" We find within the third chapter of Genesis, just that happening.

Another thing I want you to note about the third chapter of Genesis is the name which is used consistently throughout it for the Lord. You note as in Genesis 2, that throughout Genesis 3, it is "Jehovah God", "the Lord God" that is used. The significant exception is that Satan refuses to call Him "the Lord God". The only term that Satan uses for the Lord is "God". He refuses to name Jehovah. You will also note another significant exception, that the woman also does not name Him as Jehovah, although you will note that in Genesis 4, in the first few verses, she says, "I have gotten a man with the help of Jehovah." For the name was known to Eve, evidently, but when she is speaking with the devil, she does not use the name of Jehovah. She also refers to Him as God.

I think there you have the key to the conflict. The Lord is revealing Himself as Jehovah: God of life, God who bowed in an intimate, personal, and direct way in covenant relationship with His people. It is this that Satan is out to destroy. Satan knows only too well that a people in a covenant relationship with God cannot be destroyed. If you stay on the ground of God's covenant, you cannot be destroyed. Get off the ground of God's covenant and you will be destroyed instantaneously or be submerged and taken away. Satan knew very well the thing he had to strike was the whole relationship of God to man and man to God. He has to destroy God's covenant relationship with man. That is the obvious lesson that we learn from this chapter. In the midst of failure, in the midst of sorrow, and in the midst of complete breakdown, we find that the Lord comes in as Jehovah, Jehovah God, known throughout. It would be a terrible thing to be known as Jehovah God in Genesis 2 and as just God in Genesis 3. But the most wonderful thing of all is that the Lord reveals himself in Genesis 3 as Jehovah God—right the way through, from beginning to end, and the exception is the devil himself.

The Craftiness of the Devil

Now let's take a closer look at this chapter. (I do trust you do not find this too heavy.) The first thing I want you to look at more closely is the fall itself. Let us see what we can learn from the fall. I do not believe that the devil's method changes. Although the devil has been at work for thousands and thousands and thousands of years, his methods do not change. You are going to find, if you are anything like me, that the way the devil came to Eve, and the way he worked, is very much the same as the way he comes to you and to me.

First of all, I want you to note this: mark the devil's craftiness. Now, if we were planning a strategy, I am quite sure we would have done something quite different, but mark the devil's strategy. He takes a serpent, which is a subject creature to man, under God's order. Through the serpent he comes to woman, through woman he gets at man, and through man he gets at the Lord. I wonder what would have happened if he had started with man? I wonder what would have happened if he had started with the Lord? The devil evidently had his stratagem and he began with the serpent, and he mastered the serpent first. Evidently, he got control of the serpent in some way or other, and through this, the woman. She did not think for a moment because it says, quite clearly, in the Word of God that Eve was deceived, but it also says clearly that Adam was not deceived. He took deliberately, whereas

Eve was deceived when she took. The serpent came then to Eve, and by that method, the enemy deceived, beguiled Eve, so that she did take. Then, by the woman, the man came and also took. Thus, the enemy had won the day, as it were. That is very interesting, because I have found in my own experience—I am sure you have found in yours—that we hardly ever fall from frontal attacks.

Working Through Innocent Things

When the enemy comes in with a terrific onslaught, we know that it is the enemy. We flee for refuge, but is it not true that the enemy often comes through innocent things? The woman must have told herself that it was a perfectly innocent creature. She was quite evidently used to it in the garden. We have talked about the fact that she was not surprised about its speech. But evidently, whatever it was, this was quite innocent. She never thought for a moment that anything satanic was coming out of this. It was something that was perfectly normal in her life, something, furthermore, which was part of the whole relationship of man to the animal creation. Man had dominion; man had been placed in relationship to those creatures. He was to watch over them, to tend them, and so on. He was supposed to dress and keep the garden and everything in it. It must have been very, very interesting that somehow that was the way it came. Then the enemy got to Adam through his wife. Perhaps if the enemy had come himself, I do not know, Adam maybe would have been more on his guard, but coming as he did to his wife, he was caught off guard.

Planting the Seed of Doubt

There are other things than that simple craftiness of the devil. Note how simply the serpent says some things. You see the first thing in verse one: "Yea, hath God said ye shall not eat of any tree of the garden?" There are three things we find about how the enemy opens his conversation. First of all, he plants the seed of doubt. He says in a very winning way, "Did God say that? Did you hear right? Are you absolutely sure that God said you are not to eat anything in the garden?" Mark carefully what he said. He was very, very clever. He planted a seed by telling a lie. He said, "Yea, hath God said ye shall not eat of any tree or all the trees of the garden?" The Lord never said that and never meant that either. He was using two other ways. First of all, it was false innocence, and that is always a method of the enemy. He comes at you, he talks to you, and, sometimes, through your own thoughts, says, "Hath God told us …?" He always just gives a twist to things, which of course, the Lord never said. The Lord never said you shall not eat of every tree or all the trees from the garden. What the Lord said was: "Of the tree of knowledge of good and evil thou shall not eat of it."

The first thing Satan does is plant a doubt. Could a God of love, a God of goodness, a God of grace, and a God of mercy really suggest anything like this? "Yea, hath God said?" He did it, not by saying in a mocking voice, "Yea hath God said you shall not eat of any?" I think, possibly, Eve would have been a little more on her guard. Don't you see? The way he did it was by assuming ignorance: "Instruct me. I don't know about this. I'm very, very ignorant of these things. I'm quite innocent. I need a little bit of your help. Could you please tell me? Surely, He didn't say you shouldn't eat any of the fruit!" Of course Eve walks into the trap. He wins her confidence by stirring her pride. She began to tell him straightway, "Oh no," she said, "you've got it wrong! The Lord never said we couldn't eat of the trees of the garden, but He said we should not eat of that tree." But he had won her confidence, not her guard. That is always the way the enemy comes to us, always. Pride or vanity is always the ground for failure. While there is a vestige of vanity left in us, it will become, in the end, our downfall. It is why the Lord has to take such pains to smash our pride in us.

Some of you wonder: Why does the Lord show me how vile I am? Why does He continually show me how sinful and all the rest of it? Because He's got to smash this thing that we call pride. Leave a pocket of it, and it is ground for the enemy. Along that line, he will always come. "Oh, I'll just somehow get in your confidence, you see." It's quite innocent.

Well, that is the first thing I want you to note about the devil. You see, he talks of all the trees when he knew very well it was one tree. He assumes an ignorance and an innocence about the whole thing. Then he wins the confidence by putting himself in the place of, being instructed. He said, "Now tell me." Never talk with the devil! The Scripture never told us anywhere to talk with the devil. It says, "Resist the devil and he will flee from you." If you parlay with the devil, you are lost and here you have it, you see. If only Eve had said straightway, "No I'm not talking about that!" But no, she started to talk, and in a sense, the devil knew what the end was going to be. He had won her confidence.

Mixing Truth with Lies

The second thing I want you to notice is the way the devil mixes truth with lies. You see, all the time the devil was mixing in truth with a lie. He says, "Yea, hath God said, Ye shall not eat of any tree of the garden?" Well, that's a lie and yet, you know, it's true. He has mixed in truth with a lie. A little farther on he says, "Ye shall not surely die: for God doth know that in the day ye eat thereof, then your eyes shall be opened, and ye shall be as God, knowing good and evil." There is truth and there is lie there. It's a mixture. The enemy is very, very clever. He never comes along the lines of complete falsehood; he comes along the lines of a mixture. He is like an angel of light, like a minster of righteousness. That is the way he comes along. Always. Every time.

Contradicting God

Then I want you to notice another thing. Having come that far with Eve, he now feels he can take a further step, and we come to this in verse 4 and 5: "Ye shall not surely die," he says. That is not a question. He doesn't say "You shall not surely die?" He said, "You shall not surely die!" He says it quite certainly: "you'll not die." We find a further few things. First of all, we find Satan blatantly contradicts God. Blatantly contradicts God! Whenever anything blatantly contradicts God, we know where it comes from. It is amazing how often in our experience something blatantly contradicts God. Here it is in the Word of God, but some people will say, "No, that is not so! That is not so. That is not the truth!" It is amazing how we find that again and again.

Another thing, of course, is that the devil told a lie. The Lord Jesus said he is the father of lies. He is a liar from the beginning. He told a lie: "Ye shall not surely die."

The other, and I think the most remarkable, thing is that he makes a charge (and I cannot find a word really to describe it) of meanness against the Lord. What he was saying to Eve was simply this: "Look here, Eve, you won't die. This is stupid! You won't die! He only told you that. The reason He told you, He threatened you with death, is simply that He is frightened that you will get elevated. He knows very well that if you do the thing He says you must not do, you will be immediately elevated. You will come into a position, which is on equality with God. You will be there, as it were, as God. You won't need Him! You will be independent of God and you will be able to live a life of independence."

It's amazing, really, when you think of the way that the enemy always comes along. I know this must answer something in many of your lives because many of you have spoken along this very line. One of the greatest things the Lord has to do with us is to get rid of this perverted idea of God that is somehow born inside of us. We have the idea, and it is one of our greatest difficulties when it comes to the Lordship of Christ, that God is avaricious, that He will take everything and give nothing. That He will grind us into the dust. He will make us little servile slaves that have absolutely nothing, living lives that are miserable, joyless, empty, and vacuous. You know that kind of feeling we all get: "Oh, if I do that, if I go along that way, do you know what the Lord will do to me? He will take everything. He will give nothing. He is so mean. He is not really out for my best. He wants to take away my career from me. He wants to smash up my home, or to take away my own desires. He wants to sort of stop me getting any place, stop me from getting at all satisfied. He wants everything for Himself! He does not want me to have anything."

That is just the charge that Satan made with Eve. He said, "Eve, if you only knew what He was like. He's avaricious. He's mean. He only threatened you because He's so afraid that if you take that line, He will lose a lot. You won't need Him anymore. You'll be independent." You could see that. It's truth, and it's a lie. There's a sense in which it is true. Let man take that course and he will be independent of God. At the same time, little did Eve realise everything that was bound up with taking that course. She may be independent of God, but what else came in by that independence of God? What about all the sorrow, and misery, and death, and corruption, and degradation, and all the rest to which she opened the floodgates at that time? Well, there you have something very, very remarkable because it is so true that Satan still works along these very lines. These are the lines upon which he comes, again and again to us. He speaks to us along these lines. He gets at us along these lines.

Use of the Name Jehovah

Finally, you will note that he never uses the name of Jehovah. No wonder. He could not offer Jehovah the name and then charge the Lord with meanness and avarice. Jehovah must be kicked as far out of the vicinity of the woman as possible. He could only speak of Him as God—great God, distant God, mighty and grand, all-powerful. That is all he could speak of and he did not bring in once that relationship of Jehovah.

Then look at the woman, and you will see immediately in verse two her undoing. She leaves the ground of covenant and she calls Him just "God." That is the beginning of it all. When Satan started talking with her, the poison had worked already. She forgot the Lord, in His love, and in His grace, and in His relationship to man; she was not seeing that.

Then you will notice another thing about the woman—the absence of fellowship. She had no fellowship about the matter. She acted very, very hastily indeed. The devil spoke to her: "Come on. I mean, surely," he says, "a good God of grace and love wouldn't require this kind of thing or put this kind of restriction on you, would He?" Of course, later on he comes right out in the open and he says, "Of course he wouldn't. It's a lie! He knows very well that if you take that it's finished. You will come into a new, released, liberated and emancipated sphere, where you will be just, rather like Him!" You see, she did not talk about it. She just looked at herself. The devil is always using methods, and his lie has not really changed all that much. His lie is more or less the same—has been the same from the beginning. He always promises the same things. Even today, he is promising to make people as gods.

You know about the absence of fellowship; there is the absence of order, too. Where is she? It is very, very interesting. Eve fell in this way and she did something which she should not have done. She took a very big step, didn't she? Very hastily, spur of the moment. Well, we do feel that her husband should have been leading in the matter, but he wasn't. Eve was in the lead in the matter.

Then you will notice another thing, which is rather remarkable. Compare what Eve said that the Lord said, and what the Lord actually said. The Lord actually said, "Of every tree of the garden, thou mayest freely eat; but of the tree of the knowledge of good and evil, thou shalt not eat of it: for in the day that thou eatest thereof thou shalt surely die" (Genesis 2:16–17). This is what Eve said: "Of the fruit of the trees of the garden we may eat. But of the fruit of the tree which is in the midst of the garden, God has said, 'Ye shall not eat of it, neither shall ye touch it lest you die.'"

You will see an interesting thing there. This is the way the devil always works with us, he tones down God's richness. Instead of having this in her mind: "of every tree of the garden thou may freely eat"— Eve evidently has gotten toned down to this: "of the trees of the garden you may eat. But of the fruit of the tree which is in the midst of the garden, God has said, 'Ye shall not eat of it, neither shall ye touch it ...'" That may have been very good and very true. She was taught not to eat it and it is best not to touch it either.[1]

---

1 We apologise, the last ten minutes of the audio from this study was missing.

6.
The Consequences of the Fall

Genesis 3

Now the serpent was more subtle than any beast of the field which Jehovah God had made. And he said unto the woman, Yea, hath God said, Ye shall not eat of any tree of the garden?

And the woman said unto the serpent, Of the fruit of the trees of the garden we may eat: but of the fruit of the tree which is in the midst of the garden, God hath said, Ye shall not eat of it, neither shall ye touch it, lest ye die. And the serpent said unto the woman, Ye shall not surely die: for God doth know that in the day ye eat thereof, then your eyes shall be opened, and ye shall be as God, knowing good and evil. And when the woman saw that the tree was good for food, and that it was a delight to the eyes, and that the tree was to be desired to make one wise, she took of the fruit thereof, and did eat; and she gave also unto her husband with her, and he did eat. And the eyes of them both were opened, and they knew that they were naked; and they sewed fig-leaves together, and made themselves aprons. And they heard the voice of Jehovah God walking in the garden in the cool of the day: and the man and his wife hid themselves from the presence of Jehovah God amongst the trees of the garden.

And Jehovah God called unto the man, and said unto him, Where art thou? And he said, I heard thy voice in the garden, and I was afraid, because I was naked; and I hid myself. And he said, Who told thee that thou wast naked? Hast thou eaten of the tree, whereof I commanded thee that thou shouldest not eat? And the man said, The woman whom thou gavest to be with me, she gave me of the tree, and I did eat. And Jehovah God said unto the woman, What is this thou hast done? And the woman said, The serpent beguiled me, and I did eat. And Jehovah God said unto the serpent, Because thou hast done this, cursed art thou above all cattle, and above every beast of the field; upon thy belly shalt thou go, and dust shalt thou eat all the days of thy life: and I will put enmity between thee and the woman, and between thy seed and her seed: he shall bruise thy head, and thou shalt bruise his heel. Unto the woman he said, I will greatly multiply thy pain and thy conception; in pain thou shalt bring forth children; and thy desire shall be to thy husband, and he shall rule over thee. And unto Adam he said, Because thou hast hearkened unto the voice of thy wife, and hast eaten of the tree, of which I commanded thee, saying, Thou shalt not eat of it: cursed is the ground for thy sake; in toil shalt thou eat of it all the days of thy life; thorns also and thistles shall it bring forth to thee; and thou shalt eat the herb of the field; in the sweat of thy face shalt thou *eat bread, till thou return unto the ground; for out of it wast thou taken: for dust thou art, and unto dust shalt thou return. And the man called his wife's name Eve; because she was the mother of all living. And Jehovah God made for Adam and for his wife coats of skins, and clothed them.*

And Jehovah God said, Behold, the man is become as one of us, to know good and evil; and now, lest he put forth his hand, and take also of the tree of life, and eat, and live for ever— therefore Jehovah God sent him forth from the garden of Eden, to till the ground from whence he was taken. So he drove out the man; and he placed at the east of the garden of Eden the Cherubim, and the flame of a sword which turned every way, to keep the way of the tree of life.

We have said that this chapter, Genesis 3, is the explanation of the present. Genesis 1 is the fact of creation, Genesis 2 is the purpose of creation, and Genesis 3 is the explanation of the present. What has happened? What has happened to God's wonderful, glorious purpose and destiny for man? Why this mess? When God has said that all things are so good, why is there so much evil? Why the disharmony and so on?

We will not go back over that, but you will remember one thing about Genesis chapter 3: the very first few words introduce an altogether new element. We have hardly entered into chapter 3, when we are in the presence of Satan for the first time, as far as these three chapters go. Someone new comes onto the scene. As far as we knew, if we were to go only by Genesis 1 and 2, we would not have known this evil being existed. We did not know there was any antagonism, that there was any adversary. Now we are in the presence of someone who is obviously a violent antagonist of God.

One of the things that we said last time was that chapter 3 is a background of a ferocious hatred of God, and particularly of Christ, and man as related to Christ. The one significant thing about chapter 3 is the way God is named. Throughout the whole chapter He is called the Lord God, Jehovah God, bringing into view the simple fact of His love and the whole desire of His heart to be in intimate, personal, and direct union with His people. The devil, significantly enough, never ever allows that name to come upon his lips. He only refers to Him as God: "Yea, hath God said?" and so on. The woman falls when she leaves the ground of that relationship to the Lord and says, "God hath said." You have there the key to the conflict: there is an antagonist of God and he is out to destroy everything that really is satisfying to God. He is out not only to destroy it, but in many ways to seduce it and then to possess it himself.

Spiritual Conflict

Thus, you see, human history is really but the theatre of a tremendous, invisible, spiritual conflict. There are two tremendous forces and these forces are out to possess humanity. On the one side you have God and His purpose, and on the other side you have the one that we call "that old serpent." Some people think that is very far-fetched, but I think when we go a little further into it, we are going to see that it is not the least bit far-fetched at all. It is not even fantastic. It is borne out amply in our own experience and life. Here then, whilst Genesis 3 only very, very simply, clearly, and directly speaks about something of the fall and of the background of the fall, we are in a far, far greater context. Only farther on in the Bible do we discover the context of a being who left his first estate and said that he would be God and that he would exalt his throne; exalt himself to the throne of God. Then there is the whole story of his mastery of man and of the tragic results that came out of his mastery. So you see, Genesis 3 comprehends all that with these simple words: "Now the serpent." All that is gathered up in those first few words, "Now the serpent." From that we have just the simple introduction of the whole evil history of Lucifer.

You will remember that previously, we confined ourselves, to the first eight verses of this chapter, and I trust you found it helpful. We studied together something of the fall of humanity. We cannot go over that, it is far too complicated. It is not even easy to put it in a few words, but I think that most of you will have found out how the enemy always uses somewhat of the same method. The way his temptations come, the insinuations he makes, the suggestions that he makes, the suspicions he casts upon God and upon God's handiwork and God's purpose, are all here in seed form in Genesis 3. I do not suppose there is a temptation that is common to anyone of us that is not found here in seed form. Somewhere in these few verses from 1–8, it is all comprehended—the whole stratagem of the evil one, the way that he comes at us.

I want to go straight on now to this one point: the consequences of the fall. We dealt with the actual fall previously. What were the consequences of the fall? What happened as a result of the fall? Exactly what happened? Here we are, as it were, at the point of an explanation. We are told simply, that the explanation of why everything is in disharmony, and why everything is not "very good" as God originally made it, and why God's purpose seems utterly to have failed, is because man has fallen. Something has happened, and man has been displaced; he has left his position. The result has been a catastrophe of the very first rate. But the consequences of the fall are far more instructive. It is one thing, as we often hear in gospel messages, to hear that the fall is the answer to everything in one way, and that it is the explanation of everything. People say, "Ah, man was born." They will talk in terms of what they call 'original sin' and they will say this is the explanation of everything. Well, that is one thing but it is not very satisfying is it? We have to understand what the fall meant, and what were the consequences of it.

Man's Constitution Changed

The first thing we find, and it is a very, very important thing, is that man's constitution is totally different from the one God intended. Now, that goes right back to Genesis 2. God constituted man in a certain way. Man was constituted along a certain line. He was made for a certain purpose, with a certain goal in view. Was man made at the beginning a spiritual person? Well, the Scripture seems quite clear: man was made at the beginning a *potentially* spiritual person. God's whole thought in man's constitution was that he was of a spiritual constitution. His first natural condition was but the probation of something far more wonderful.

Man's whole constitution is made in such a way as to be very dissatisfied with the natural. He cannot settle down to it. When Adam was first made, he was made, according to the Scripture, a living soul. He must have been conscious of the fact that, whilst he was perfect, whilst he was sinless, whilst he was innocent, there was a lack. That comes out, of course, from the question of naming the animals and the provision of his wife. But later on, it was even more obvious; it is something which I am going to answer later. Why was Eve herself conscious of a lack? She was obviously conscious of a lack. She would not have thought about that tree if she were not conscious of her lack. There was something else stirring inside her which said this is all very wonderful, all very wonderful, but is this all? Well, the point was, the devil was telling her a half-truth. It was not all. God had so created Adam and Eve that they were made to be in union with God, and their only satisfaction lay in being one with God.

Now, you know what happened when God put them on probation. There is what we call the tree of life and there is what we call the tree of the knowledge of good and evil. On the one side we are offered one type of person. On the other, there is another type of person. The first type is a God-conscious man, a God-centred man, and a God-dependent man. That was the type of man that God intended. On the other, we have the tree of the knowledge of good and evil: a self-conscious, self-centred, and self-dependent type of man. Man simply chose the second. He wanted to be free from God and he wanted to be in charge of his own destiny. He wanted self-determination and he wanted to be able to live on an equality with God—very much like many people do today. People today, of course, condescend to worship God now and again, or pay Him a visit now and again, or give Him a few pennies or shillings now and again, but that is as far as it goes.

Man wanted that type of life. He wanted to be able to run his own life and determine his own course, be able to be master of his own destiny and fate, and, at the same time, be able to treat God as an equal. This was what the devil said to man: "You will be on an equality. You will not be riveted to God. You won't be dependent on God" and man said, "That's what I want. I think that could be the thing that will satisfy me."

Of course, you know the enemy made the suggestion of God's avarice: "God is avaricious, God is mean. He wants to hold you in servile bondage. He wants to make you a slave. He wants to make you the doormat for His feet, but He won't let you rise above that station. That is all He wants you for."

Man's response was, "Yes, there seems to be something to that. I do not want that kind of life under the feet of God. I do not want to be the servant of God, the slave of God. I don't want that. I want to be a person in my own right". Man chose what he thought was his emancipation and freedom, what he thought was going to be equality with God.

That is all bound up in the two trees—the tree of life and the tree of the knowledge of good and evil. The tree of life stands for God's life, and being utterly centred in God and dependent on God. The tree of the knowledge of good and evil—having the idea inside of you so that you could decide and determine and discriminate and do exactly what you thought. So we see something very, very interesting. It is a very interesting thought, whether God's idea was that, if man would have only taken the tree of life first, the tree of the knowledge of good and evil would have been open to him. If only he would have come to utter dependence upon God, God would have given him the capacity to discriminate by the spirit of God.

Man's Self-Conscious Constitution

What was the result of man's choosing of the tree of knowledge? You have it almost immediately in verses 7, 8, and 10:

> And the eyes of them both were opened, and they knew that they were naked; and they sewed fig-leaves together, and made themselves aprons. And they heard the voice of Jehovah God walking in the garden in the cool of the day: and the man and his wife hid themselves from the presence of Jehovah … And he said, I heard thy voice in the garden, and I was afraid, because I was naked; and I hid myself.

What was the very first result of man's choice? The very first evidence was of a self-conscious constitution. He suddenly became conscious of himself. He had never been conscious before of being naked. But the first thing, as soon as he chose to be that type of man, was that a self-consciousness enveloped him and destroyed all his peace of mind. He fled amongst the trees. Now, that may be putting it in a very simple way, but self-consciousness is one of the most amazing and fundamental roots of all kinds of trouble and unhappiness. It is a fundamental thing in humanity. We grow up with self-consciousness. It comes out in all kinds of ways, whether it be fear of people, fear of talking to people, fear of being yourself, or fear of God, fear of praying, all kinds of fear. Self-consciousness is a very big thing. It is not just being afraid to play the piano in the presence of friends. It is not just blushing a little if someone should mention you publicly. Self-consciousness is much deeper than that because self-consciousness is the thing that gives rise to fear and distrust.

The immediate effect of self-consciousness was fear. He was frightened of God and he would also have been frightened of other men if there had been any. It was self-consciousness that gripped him and has gripped humanity ever since. Why, the evidence of the kind of constitution we have, is self-consciousness. Look into your own heart and life and you will find that there is this thing that we call self-consciousness. It is one of the first things we find here.

Man's Self-Dependent Constitution

The second thing we find is also quite immediate: "They sewed fig leaves together and made themselves aprons." The second thing we see about this constitution was immediate. If they had taken the tree of life they would have fled to God in the presence of evil. They would have fled to God. But now, for the first time, they stand apart from God. They do not refer to Him; they do not defer to Him. They immediately start upon seeking to rectify the wrong themselves. That is the whole course of human history comprehended. The history of humanity has been trying to rectify what happened at the fall. People are always living under a kind of veneer. It is a very thin veneer, but there we are with the whole of modern society today, for instance. It is the artificial façade over a complete inner corruption. Trying, somehow, to cover it up. Trying, somehow, to gloss over it. Trying, somehow, to dress it up in one way or another and make it all seem far less evil than it really is. "It is not really that. Don't call sin, *sin*. Don't call evil, *evil*. Don't call iniquity, *iniquity*. Those are just wrong thoughts, or, you know, wrong thinking or error or one or two other little thoughts along that line."

That is the kind of thing that the world says today. You must not call anything by its name. If you are in a scrape, you must get out of it. It is amazing when we come to the Lord isn't it, how this temptation is the one that commonly assails us. "You must not come to the Lord," something says to us, "You can't come to the Lord, not in that mess. You must clean yourself up before you come. You can't bring yourself like that; it's making use of God. You have to clean yourself up. You have to reform yourself and then you can come to God when you are in a slightly better condition." Well, man did just simply that. He started on the course of self-dependence and that has become one of the basic characteristics of this world. Self-consciousness is one; self-dependence is another.

Man's Self-Centred Constitution

Then you see again how self-centredness comes out quite immediately. When God says, "Hast thou eaten of the tree whereof I commanded thee that thou shouldst not eat?" Man immediately says, "The woman whom Thou gavest to be with me, she gave me of the tree, and I did eat."

When the woman was asked, she said, "The serpent beguiled me, and I did eat."

It was the first evidence of a self-centred constitution. Man now could not care less about Eve. He could not care less what happened to Eve. I do believe that if God said, "Very well, Eve must die," man would say, "That's alright, I am safe. It's very sad to see the end of Eve, but after all she did, she ought to suffer. She was the one that led me into the trouble." But it was the evidence of the self-centred constitution taking shape. Here was man, and his first thought was his own preservation. Here was woman: her first thought was her own preservation. For the first time, the constitution of man had become different. They did not think of God. They did not think of anyone else; they thought of themselves. Now, that is something upon which the whole of this world and humanity is built. So you have three things, which are the immediate result of the fall: self-consciousness, self-dependence, and self-centredness.

The Perversion of Man's Constitution

Now, that leads us to say one or two things. This means that man has a permanently disabled, perverted, and dissatisfying constitution. Self is the most disabling thing of all—a terribly disabling thing. It can take you a long way and leave you wrecked. People climb to the top of their sphere, and of their realm by self-hood, by aggressive self-hood, forceful self-hood—we call it personality. By soul force they reach the top, only, so often, they throw themselves over a bridge or under a train or something else because it doesn't satisfy. It doesn't satisfy them.

This constitution can be given everything in this world and yet, in the end, be absolutely dissatisfied. "What shall a man give in exchange for his soul? If man were to gain the whole world and lose his own soul, what would it profit him?"

So you see, here you have something which is amazing. One of the consequences of the fall is that we have all become a certain kind of humanity that God never intended. There is not a single one of us born into this humanity that does not have this constitution. People say, "Well, it's not so apparent," and that is quite true, there are degrees. There is an amazing variety. Some people are more self-centred than others. That is quite true. It is not always to the exact same degree. There is a variety of it. Some people have a much more lovable self-centredness and other people have a simply vile self-centredness. But nevertheless, the constitution is the same. You cannot get away from the constitution whether it be a multitudinous form or a tremendous variety, the actual constitution is the same and that constitution is a disabled one. It is perverted. It has within it an eternal lack and void. That is, man in his present state, and with his present constitution, can do a tremendous amount. He can gain a tremendous amount. He can go a long way, and yet, at the end, he knows he has not really arrived there. He is conscious that he has many facts, many things, he has perhaps gained many possessions, but he does not have whatever it is that this thing inside of him tells him is the *only* thing worth living for. So, there you have the constitution that is a permanently disabled one.

You only have to go out into the world and apply these facts to the world and the world to these facts, to see how this third chapter of Genesis is the purest truth that you will find. People, as I have said, have glossed it up and dressed it up. They have tried to pretend that it is not this, but, if you get behind the veneer, get down to the basic facts, this is the thing you find everywhere—perverted people, dissatisfied people, people with a lack, people with a void, people who have a vacuum inside. You will find people whose whole life is just a long history of this kind of constitution. They do not want to leave it, and yet they cannot bear it.

The Pattern of a Disabled Constitution

Another thing I want you to note is that the whole of human history is patterned, shaped, and moulded out of this constitution. That is, the whole of human history simply bears out this constitution. People say, "Why all the wars? Why the strife? Why the carnage? Why the bloodshed? Why the factions?" There you have it. You can have all the summit meetings in the world, and the treaties made, and pacts made, and conferences made, and all the rest of it, but it just lasts, literally, for as long as man's self-hood allows it. Self-hood is the thing that lies at the root of it all–whether it is national, or racial, or whatever it is, self-hood is at the root of it. It is that thing which can never give peace. That is why God says there is no peace for the wicked. They are like the restless waves of the sea. In the Scripture, the nations are often depicted as the sea roaring backwards and forwards in an eternal state of turmoil and restlessness—they can't find peace, they can't rest.

Well, there you are. You will see there that education, culture, any kind of social reform, will not touch the matter at all. You can educate and educate and educate a person, but you can never educate them out of this constitution. You can try to make a person cultured. You can instruct them. You can do every kind of thing with them, but you cannot do anything about that constitution. You can find the most cultured person who is the very symbol and personification of this kind of constitution. I will give you examples of that, of people who have been the vilest of men, the greatest of dictators, who have been, at the same time, very educated and very cultured people. We could go through history just proving these simple facts that you cannot get away from this constitution. You can educate it, you can cultivate it, you can develop it, you can try to suppress it or repress it, but you will not make a difference. The Lord Jesus has the answer: "Except a man be born again, he cannot see the kingdom of God."

Man's Alliance with Satan

I do not know whether we sufficiently realise how really terrible that first consequence of the fall is. But the second is certainly even more terrible. That is, a most profound and terrible alliance has been made between Satan and man. This is found in verse 15: "I will put enmity between thee and the woman. And between thy seed and her seed." What did the Lord mean when he said to the serpent, "Thy seed?" He was really saying that a most terrible, terrible alliance had come into being between Satan and man. A terrible alliance. I think we ought to look at some scriptures on that to bear that out.

I speak the things which I have seen with my Father: and ye also do the things which ye heard from your father. (John 8:38)

Ye do the works of your father. They said unto him, We were not born of fornication; we have one Father, even God. (John 8:41)

Ye are of your father the devil, and the lusts of your father it is your will to do. He was a murderer from the beginning, and standeth not in the truth, because there is no truth in him. When he speaketh a lie, he speaketh of his own: for he is a liar, and the father thereof. (John 8:44)

You will note: "Your father the devil." The Lord Jesus contrasts His Father with our father. "Ye are of your father," He says, "the devil."

But when he saw many of the Pharisees and Sadducees coming to his baptism, he said unto them, Ye offspring of vipers, who warned you to flee from the wrath to come? (Matthew 3:7)

Ye offspring of vipers, how can ye, being evil, speak good things? for out of the abundance of the heart the mouth speaketh. (Matthew 12:34)

... he that doeth sin is of the devil; for the devil sinneth from the beginning. To this end was the Son of God manifested, that he might destroy the works of the devil. (1 John 3:8)

We know that we are of God, and the whole world lieth in the evil one. (1 John 5:19)

Perhaps the most terrible thing about the fall is the fact that humanity has been fathered by the devil. It was not merely that

Satan seduced humanity. It was not merely that he deceived humanity. It was that in that act, humanity became involved in Satan, so that John could say, "The whole world lieth in the evil one," and so that the Lord Jesus could speak of him as the prince of this world, or age. A most terrible alliance took place at the fall. Man's self-centred constitution was fathered by the devil, so that the Scripture, from beginning to end, bears out this simple point: by birth, naturally, we are born into an alliance with the evil one and into a relationship with the evil one that involves us in ultimate judgment.

God's Judgment

God is going to judge the prince of this world and because He is going to judge and has judged the prince of this world, all that are involved with him are judged in his judgment. If you read the book of Revelation, you find that the devil will be cast into the lake of fire along with all that are not written in the Lamb's book of life—everyone that is fathered by the devil, everyone that is in this alliance with the devil, everyone that has this relationship to the devil. It is not a question of how you grow up; whether you and I say, "I think I am going to leave God to Himself." It is not that at all. It is the concept that, by birth, whether we like it or not, we are in a relationship with the devil and the only way out of that relationship is to be born again. That is the way out. You can reform, you can have a cleanup, you can become religious, you can get christened, you can be baptised, you can get confirmed, you can come and take communion here, you can do what you like, but that will not affect you. God shut the path to that way. The Scripture is quite implicit. For you and I, the only way to get out of this relationship with the devil, is to be born again, and then that link is snapped. We may know something of an old nature, of a flesh life, which is the ground for the enemy. But thank God, the Scriptures say we are of God, born not of the will of man or of the will of the flesh nor blood, but of God.

One thing that is quite clear from the Scriptures: by the fall, there came into being a relationship between humanity and the devil which never existed before. The relationship is as father to children and children to father. That is borne out far, far more deeply than I have said because the Lord takes up again and again by saying this simple thing, "The works of your father ye will do." He is just stressing a character that has been transmitted from father to son and He says the kind of works that that character produces in the father are the kind of works that are going to be produced in the family. Thus we get this: you sin, the devil sinned from the beginning; you lust, the devil lusted from the beginning; you murder because the devil murdered from the beginning; you lie because the devil lied from the beginning.

You see, the devil himself fell into this kind of constitution. This raises many problems, but it was the "I" that first came into prominence. If you read in Isaiah and Ezekiel it says, "I will be like the Most High. I will exalt my throne," and so on. It was the "I." Now, this has come into man. Man has become a different kind of constitution, and the result is a terrible relationship with Satan. You should study this. You cannot get away from it by just saying, "Is this the Pharisees and Sadducees?" because John makes it as broad as, "He that doeth sin is of the devil," and then he goes on. "This is how we can tell the children of God and the children of the devil". Then again, "The whole world lieth in the evil one." Moreover as I have already said, the judgment of the world, the judgment upon Satan, is a judgment that the whole of the devil fathered humanity is involved in.

An Alliance Maintained and Developed

Now, you may need a little more evidence for that. In the Word of God, this relationship, which came into being at the fall, is a relationship which the devil maintained and develops. If you look at Ephesians 2, and I think this is really a key thing, there's no Scripture of private interpretation. We will read from verse one because I think it bears out this point.

And you did he make alive, when ye were dead through
your trespasses and sins, wherein ye once walked according
to the course of this world, according to the prince of
the powers of the air, of the spirit that now worketh
in the sons of disobedience ... (Ephesians 2:1–2)

I want you to note three things. In verse 2, "according to," where anyone has walked "according to." What does that mean, "according to"? You walked according to whom? "To the course of this world." According to "the prince of the powers of the air." Who is the prince of the powers of the air? You and I walked according to him.

But there is something even more terrible here. It says, "The spirit that worketh in the sons of disobedience." You know what the word "worketh" is? It is the word "energises." He energises them. He is the force in them, the life force, the power. There is not one of us who is excluded. We were all children of wrath. Children of wrath is a term that is synonymous with "children of the devil," "children of the night," "children of darkness," it says, and so on. It is just one aspect of it: children of wrath.

Will you note another thing? You note "according to," and "worketh in," energises, and the other is "sons of disobedience." That word does not say "children," we are children of God. What are sons? They are those that have gone forward. So then Satan maintains this relationship, as the Lord maintains His relationship with us in new birth. As He tries to bring us to the point of fellowship, so Satan brings his children to be full-blooded sons of disobedience—not just children, but responsible, quite responsible, a grown-up in evil, a grown-up in disobedience. Now Satan is absolutely energising them. I say, that is a tremendous thing; something which perhaps we can only grasp very, very, very simply. So you see, Satan's character is reproduced.

If you look at John 8:44, you will find these things. "... the lusts of your father it is your will to do. He was a murderer from the beginning, and standeth not in the truth, because there is no truth in him. When he speaketh a lie, he speaketh of his own: for he is a liar, and the father thereof." What does that simply mean? There are three things there—lust, murder, and lies. And those three things are basic constituents of this age and of this humanity. You know, murder does not necessarily mean literally actual murder. The Lord Jesus told us that. It is the spirit of the thing. You can murder the person without actually killing them. This world is also a lie. It is built in a lie, built on a lie. The whole structure is false.

So you see, there is a most terrible consequence of the fall. We have not only got a constitution that is so different from what God meant it to be, but one which can never bring us joy or happiness. It must forever leave us disabled and dissatisfied, because we have come into a relationship with the enemy. Oh! You and I only find out when we are saved, how strong an alliance our flesh has got with Satan. It would side with him so many times. It would do his will. It would flee to him if it could. Oh, people say, "This is a bit far-fetched and fantastic." But oh, when you find out what you are like, you can find out what an alliance there is with your flesh life and the enemy, even when we are children of God. Look at Romans 7:24, the great contortion of a child of God when he begins to find out that there is something in him, He calls, "Oh, wretched man that I am! who can deliver me from the body of this death?" There is something here that has got an alliance with evil powers, with evil things. Like the raven, it must satisfy itself with those things. So, there is something terrible.

The Perversion of God's Character in Man's Eyes

A third consequence of the fall is a subtle perversion of God's character and purpose in the eyes of man. Already, we have seen the beginning of this in the perversion of Eve. How she began to entertain doubts about God's goodness, and liberality, and God's love and grace and so on. Gradually, as that developed, the enemy piled on the insinuations, until, in the end, he deliberately contradicted God in a quite blatant way. Then Eve succumbs to the whole thing.

One of the most tragic things about our natural state is the perversion of God's character. We either have this view of a God that terrifies us or we have this other view of a God that is so benign that He never wants sorrow and who will let you do anything and get away with it. Neither are true. It is a terrible, terrible work of Satan, this terrible work of perverting God's character in man's eyes.

You see it here straightway in Genesis 3, the terror with which man viewed God. He really was immediately terrified of Him. A fear had come in. A terror. A distrust of God. Man could not trust God in the same way that he had trusted Him before. He fled from Him. He wondered just what was going to happen and exactly how things were going to work out and that has been so ever since in that way. It is amazing when people first come under the sound of the gospel. They are so afraid. They cannot trust the Lord. They are quite sure that if they go that way it is going to be terribly miserable.

You find this work of the enemy in the Scripture quite clearly. The Lord Jesus summed it up when He spoke to the woman at the well of Samaria. In John 4:22, He said, "Ye worship that which ye know not." What an amazing phrase that was. "Ye worship that which ye know not." Then again, it comes out in II Corinthians 4:4, "The god of this age hath blinded the minds of them that believe not, lest they should see." You worship that which you know not. Do you know what you are worshiping? You do not. Well, I suppose you are worshipping the god of this age. He deceived the minds of those that do not believe.

Again, people say, "That's too far, that's going too far," but just wait, we have to investigate these things to see if we are going far enough. In Romans 1:21–23, we have this: "... because that knowing God, they glorified him not as God, neither gave thanks; but became vain in their reasonings, and their senseless heart was darkened. Professing themselves to be wise they became fools, and changed the glory of the incorruptible God for the likeness of an image of corruptible man, and of birds, and four-footed beasts, and creeping things." In other words, so terrible did this perversion of God's character become that man began to worship the "weird side." You only need to see pictures of some of the idols in places like India or Burma or some of the other southeast nations to realise what weird things man will worship. You see something with a thousand arms, and a nose that comes up, or jagged teeth, or bulbous eyes, or things that are terrible in the extreme, and then you think this is far-fetched? How could man come to worship such a perversion of God's character? Some of the idols in Hindu India have bodies that hang out of the mouth, carved, hanging out of the mouth—gods that have people clutched in their hands, feeding themselves, and men bow down and give offerings of rice and other things to such creatures. Well, it is all contained here in this amazing verse 25, "for that they exchanged the truth of God for a lie, and worshipped and served the creature rather than the Creator ..." You then read the rest, of how God gave them up to all kinds of terrible things.

Do you see what happens? This perversion of God's character in the eyes of men has the most far-reaching consequences. It meant that man went down to a degraded and depraved level to do all kinds of things because, you see, what you worship has a tremendous effect upon the standard of your life. It is a tremendous thing. Worship an idol and you will find that out.

You will find it again in Paul's great argument in 1 Corinthians 10:19–20a, "What say I then? That the things sacrificed to idols is anything, or that an idol is anything? But I say, that the things which the Gentiles sacrifice, they sacrifice to demons." So there you have it. Behind the idol—demons. All kinds of things are perpetrated in the name of God by the god of this age. Men and women, in countries not only in the east, but here in the west, are gripped in a vice-like grip of a worship, which they believe to be of God, when it is demonic. We find that again and again in all kinds of ways.

Man's Separation from God

Another consequence of the fall was an awful separation from God. A separation from God, which, as you know, had its beginning in man's fear of God. He fled from God, but later on, God shut him out. He drove him out of the garden of Eden. This separation between God and man is not just judicial, as some people think. It is something far, far more practical than a judicial, legal separation. Man lost the only constitution by which he could be one with God. That is the point. There was no good in God keeping man in a state of abject misery in His presence. Man, in the presence of God, in his present constitution, is in abject misery. God was merciful in driving man out from the garden and putting that flame of a sword that cut every way to stop man from ever getting back, until something could happen in a way that could restore man in a right way. It was not just a judicial separation, a legal separation. It was a separation that came about because man was no longer capable of being one with God. He had lost the capacity. That, I say, is a terrible thing! It is far, far, far more practical than we realise.

You get all these things that we find in the world: aimlessness, valuelessness, emptiness, fretfulness, and so on. From where do they come? They come from a creature that was made for its God but that is away from Him. That separation in Scripture is simply called death. You see, death in the eyes of God is not cessation of being. We always think of death as cessation of being, the annihilation of something, the end, the eliminating of something. Death, in the eyes of God, is something which has ceased to function as it should, or ceased to have the capacity to fulfil the ministry that it should. That is death. It is something that is made for a certain purpose that is now no good.

Think of a glass tumbler. If it were here, I would say, "Here is a tumbler that was made to hold water. It is alive because it is fulfilling its capacity to me. I want a drink, and there it is fulfilling its ministry, its purpose. There is its destiny, being fulfilled." If I take the bottom out, I might look at it and think: It is there, but what use is it? As far as I am concerned it is dead, utterly dead! It cannot even be satisfied itself, because it can never fulfil that for which it was created. That is death in the sight of God. Man is dead because he has lost the only constitution which made him capable of being one with God. So, I think you see how terrible those consequences are.

The Breakdown of all Man's Relationships

There are just one or two other effects of the fall that I would lump together. One is the breakdown in all man's relationships. It was immediate. What was once harmonious and co-operative, related, and interdependent became now all broken up. His relationship with God snapped. His relationship with woman snapped. He blamed her straightway. His relationship with the animal creation snapped. You will see it quite clearly here. For the first time, an animal had to die for the sake of man in this chapter. You have also here, even his relationship with the vegetable creation, or the plant creation, if you want to call it that, has collapsed. Instead of being in harmony with him, it is somehow against him almost. It has to be coerced and beaten to produce anything or for him to get anywhere with it. It causes him sorrow, toil, and labour, and by the sweat of his brow he lives by it. So you see all his relationships have broken down.

Immediately in Genesis 4, man's relationship with other men has broken down. In the first few verses, Abel is slain by Cain. In the last few verses of chapter 4, Lamech kills two men—the first few verses and the last few verses of it. So man's relationships with men are broken down, and that begins the whole history of the breakdown of human relationship in every field, whether it be with God, with woman, between the sexes, whether between man and man or woman and woman, whether it be social, national, international, racial, whatever it is. It is the story of the breakdown of human relationships on every side. It is the breakdown of relationships with creatures. You come to Genesis 9, and then God allowed the terrible dread and fear of man to come upon the animal creation. It is the outworking of something, all the time, the breakdown, in an ever-increasing way, of relationships. What a terrible thing has happened by this fall. Man is not left in relationship with anything for long. It is a struggle to keep in any kind of relationship because of this terrible breakdown.

You see also that the natural creation is perverted. In Romans 8:19–22, you find the wonderful words about the whole creation groaning and travailing in pain together until now. What are they waiting for? They are waiting for the wonderful emancipation from this bondage to corruption. What does it all wait for? It waits for the revealing of the sons of God. When the sons of God are revealed, and that means when man is back in his place, with God at the heart of everything, then everything else will come back into its harmony and relatedness once more. Isn't that a very wonderful thing? But because man has fallen, the natural creation itself is all out of gear. We find this all the way through the wonderful prophecies of Isaiah when he said the leopard shall lie down with the kid and the wolf with the lamb. The child shall play with the adder and also with the asp, and so on. Those are wonderful, wonderful glimpses of the future when everything once more is back in its old condition of harmony and relatedness. Well, that is something very, very wonderful there.[1]

---

1 We apologise, the last ten minutes of the audio from this study was missing.

7.
Genesis
Study Guide

Introduction

The name "Genesis" means "origin" or "generation" (Greek, from Septuagint LXX). The Hebrew title is taken from Gen 1:1, "In the beginning ..."

Genesis is also called "The First Book of Moses, or "The First Book of the Law". The Law (Hebrew, *Torah*) consists of the five books of the Pentateuch. The five books were meant to be read as one volume.

Genesis has been called the "seed-plot of the Bible"—all that is developed later, right through to The Revelation of Jesus Christ is found here in embryo.

Genesis has been subjected to much destructive criticism from unbelieving sources. If Satan can undermine faith in this first book of the Bible, then, to a large extent, faith has been undermined in the whole Word of God. This book is fundamental in every sense, and it is not surprising that Satan, the father of lies (John 8:44), should seek to destroy it.

Authorship and Date

It would be more strictly correct to use the term "editorship," rather than authorship. From the evidence, it would seem that Moses edited or compiled Genesis.

Moses obviously used very old sources for Genesis. These were possibly records brought by Abraham from Babylonia, records written by the patriarchs themselves, on clay tablets, which later came into the possession of Moses. These ancient records are separated by the recurrent phrase: "These are the generations of ..." e.g. 2:4, 5:1, 6:9, 10:1, 11:10, 11:27, 25:12, 25:19, 36:1, 37:2. (Compare also *The Documentary Theory*, which tries to explain the combination of different records, i.e. the "E tradition" using the name Elohim, and the "J tradition" using the name Yahweh etc.)

It is also interesting to note that there are many Babylonian-type names in the first 11 chapters, and many Egyptian-type names in the last 14.

All this probably means that Moses edited and compiled the documents written by eyewitnesses into a single history.

It should be noted that nowhere in the Old Testament is there cause to doubt that Moses was responsible for this and the other books of the Pentateuch being brought into existence. The New Testament writers state clearly that this is so, e.g. Acts 7:37–38 and, above all, we have the testimony of Jesus Christ Himself to this fact.

The Old Testament was compiled between 1400 BC (Garstang) and 1300 BC (Albright), and covers the following periods:

Adam–Abraham = 19 generations

Abraham–Joseph = 14 generations

Style

The style of Genesis is simple and concise. It is so written as to give specific truth, prophetic teaching, and historical content, in a readable fashion, enriched by details of geography, biology, and ancient law and custom.

Key to the Book

Genesis is the book of beginnings. It reveals to us the cause of everything, the generating dynamic, the origin. Remember, origin determines destiny.

Thus, we have the beginning of the universe, natural life, man, marriage, family, sin, social evil, immorality, corruption, death, the good seed, the bad seed, redemption, sacrifice, covenants, altars, languages, nations, human government, cities, the people of God. Also included are music, art, literature, agriculture, etc.

We find in Genesis the beginnings of the great themes of the Bible: God's eternal purpose, election, the cross (salvation, atonement, justification, identification, sanctification, etc.) the church, the inheritance, etc.

It marks also the beginning of so much that is antichrist: the bad seed (chapter 4), Babylon (chapter 10), Ishmaelites (chapter 16), Moabites (chapter 19), Ammonites (chapter 19), Philistines, Egypt, Assyria, Jebusites, Amorites, Girgashites, Hivites (all in chapter 10), and the Edomites (chapter 36).

Outline of the Book

It is divided into two main sections:

Genesis 1–11: Creation, fall and dispersal of man, and the emergence of a godly remnant.

Genesis 12–50: Ancestors of the chosen people, a people for God–Abraham, Isaac, Jacob, Joseph.

> *"Genesis shares with the whole Bible the characteristic that the narratives are selected, not for their interest, or political importance, but for the relation they bear to God's redemptive purpose … From the first hint of a coming Saviour and Conqueror in 3:15, we see God preparing a people to be the vehicle of His ultimate revelation of Himself to the world in love. The covenant with Abraham concerns not only his descendants, but blessing to all mankind through Abraham's seed (12:2–3, Gal 3:16)".* G.T.M.

Message of the Book

Genesis reveals God's original purpose for man (1:26), made in the image of God, and qualified to have dominion. Qualification is a matter of life relationship to God and obedient dependence upon God. Adam, the first man, is tested upon these two matters, but Satan brings about his downfall, and dominion is lost to the Adamic creation.

Christ, the Second Man (1 Corinthians 15:45, 47), the promised "seed of the woman" (Genesis 3:15), secures in Himself all the purpose of God for man, and embodies the features found in the spiritual seed of Seth, which features He imparts to those who, on eating of the tree of life (John 14:6) become incorporated into the Heavenly Man.

Man's fall, with consequent moral collapse and the loss of communion with God, is countered by the Seed of the Woman giving Himself to be The Lamb of God.

The sin of man is thus met by the intervention and salvation of God (Rom 5:20), and he is brought back, gloriously, into God's original purpose for him.

Summary of Contents

I. Beginnings (Genesis 1–4)

A. Creation (Genesis 1:1–2:3)

    1. The process–work; 6 days (Genesis 1:3–31)

    2. The end–rest; Sabbath (Genesis 2:1–3)

A. The first man (Genesis 2:4–3)

    1. His probation (Genesis 2:4–25)

    2. His fall (Genesis 3)

A. The first children (Genesis 4)

    1. Abel–the first blood sacrifices

    2. Cain–the first murderer

    3. Seth–the promised Seed

II. Race developments

(Genesis 5–11)

    A. Growth and corruption (Genesis 5–11)

        1. Line through Seth–death.

        Line through Enoch–translation (Genesis 5)

        2. Mixture of seeds (Genesis 6:1–8)

        3. Divine intervention (Genesis 6:9–12)

    B. Destruction and preservation (Genesis 6:13–9)

        1. The ark (Genesis 6:13–22)

        2. The judgment by water

        (Genesis 7–8:14) (II Peter 3:5–7)

        3. The New beginning (Genesis 8:15–9)

            a) The new covenant–rainbow

            b) The old poison

    C. Multiplication and Distribution (Genesis 10–11)

        1. The three families–the earth re-peopled (Genesis 10)

        2. The tower of Babel–confusion,

        scattering (Genesis 11:1–9)

        3. The promised seed–Shem, Abram (Genesis 11:10–32)

III. The Chosen Race

(Genesis 12–50)

    A. Abraham–the life of faith (Genesis 12–23)

        1. The obedience of faith–his call (Genesis 12–14)

        2. The covenant of faith–the inheritance

        (Genesis 15–16)

        3. The tests of faith (Genesis 17–20)

4. The fruit and triumph of faith (Genesis 21–22)

5. Possession by faith–a burying place (Genesis 23)

B. Isaac–sonship in resurrection (Genesis 21–26)

1. The birth of the son–"Laughter" (Genesis 21)

2. The sacrifice of the son–"Where is the lamb?" (Genesis 22)

3. A bride for the son–Rebekah (Genesis 24)

4. Sons by the son–Esau and Jacob (Genesis 25–26)

C. Jacob–discipline unto service (Genesis 27–36)

1. Jacob–the supplanter (Genesis 25–31)

2. Israel–a prince with God (Genesis 32–33)

3. The house of Israel (Genesis 34–36)

D. Joseph—reigning in life (Genesis 37–50)

1. Loved by his father (Genesis 37: 1–3)

2. Betrayed by his brethren (Genesis 37:4–38)

3. Trained for dominion (Genesis 38–40)

4. Exalted to the throne (Genesis 41)

5. Preserver of life (Genesis 41:45; 42–50)

Recommended Books

New Discoveries in Babylonia about Genesis
    P.J. Wiseman
Notes on Genesis
    C.H. Mackintosh
Changed into His Likeness
    Watchman Nee

Questions

1. What is the key word in the book of Genesis?

2. Look up the passages which begin with the phrase, "These are the generations of …" Make a list of the men whose genealogies are recorded.

3. Sum up the principal message of Genesis in one sentence and couple with it one Scripture from the New Testament.

4. What do you learn in chapters 1–4 about the character of God and the character of Satan?

5. What is God's interest in man, and what is Satan's interest in man?

6. What is the outstanding prophecy concerning Christ?

7. What differences can you find between the following:
a) Cain and Abel (Genesis 4)

b) Noah and his generation (Genesis 5:28–9)

c) Shem and Ham (Genesis 9:18–10:32)

d) Abraham and Lot (Genesis 13)

e) Isaac and Ishmael (Genesis 15:1–6; 16–17; 21:1–13, Galatians 4:21–31)

f) Jacob and Esau (Genesis 25:19–34; 26:34–28:9)

g) Joseph and his brothers (Genesis 37, 39–41)

8. How many covenants between God and man can you find in Genesis? Make a list of these covenants.

9. What do you learn about God from the following passages:
a) Genesis 6:5–8

b) Genesis 18:22–32, 19:15–23

c) Genesis 21:1–7

d) Genesis 45:4–15, 50:15–21

10. Name the outstanding men of faith whom you read about in Genesis who are mentioned in Hebrews 11.

11. Why is Shem important in Genesis?

8.
Exodus: Redemption and the House of God

Exodus 1:1

Now these are the names of the sons of Israel, who came into Egypt (every man and his household came with Jacob).

Exodus 40:34

Then the cloud covered the tent of meeting, and the glory of Jehovah filled the tabernacle.

Exodus 3:13

And Moses said unto God, Behold, when I come unto the children of Israel, and shall say unto them, The God of your fathers hath sent me unto you; and they shall say to me, What is his name? What shall I say unto them?

We come now to Exodus, the second part of the Pentateuch. The Pentateuch is to be looked upon not as five separate books as such, but as a five-fold volume. It was intended to be, as it were, one consecutive history from beginning to end, and each of the five parts of this one history has a very real lesson for us.

One of the interesting things that I want you to note straightway is that we have passed in this book from a man or men as individuals, and we have come now to a people. Exodus is in a different atmosphere altogether to Genesis. If some of you have been reading the book of Genesis as well as Exodus, I wonder whether you have noticed the difference in atmosphere that there is between these two parts of the Pentateuch. The first is a very much more individual thing. You have the atmosphere of the freedom of individuals. However, as soon as you get into Exodus, you are suddenly in the corporate. It is no longer the individual. Things are now related; things are now more integrated. Everything now is bound up with a people. You have therefore passed from individuals to a people.

I think you will also notice that all God's workings in Genesis were to produce a people. The beginning is a general history, with all the nations and everything else. Then God took up three men—Abraham, Isaac, and Jacob, and we have a tremendous amount of seemingly trivial domestic detail put into God's history. Instead of it all being to do with governments and races and nations as in the first 11 chapters, now it is all to do with the household of Abraham, Isaac, and Jacob. It is how Jacob's sons behaved and what they did and didn't do and all the rest of it. We begin to scratch our heads and wonder, what has gone wrong with the book of Genesis? But we find that God was out to produce a people. I might say here just in passing that God's method has never changed—never changed! I think we can say that dogmatically. God always begins with one person. This is one of the great fundamental principles of God. He always begins with one person. You will not find a movement in the Bible which does not originate in the beginning with one person. God always said, "I will make of one a nation." That is just the way of God.

Another interesting thing is that God will spend years on one person in hidden history. He will get something in that person, do something in that person, and then begin to bring others into relationship, and do something in them before He ever moves out to a people. You find then, all God's movements in the book of Genesis are towards a people. As soon as you come to the book of Exodus, you are in the presence of a people. That is rather wonderful, that even in this part of the Pentateuch, you find the same principle at work. God takes one man, Moses, (although even Moses did not know it) and prepares him for forty years. Then, He sends that man into the desert for another forty years. This time he knows he is under the hand of God, and for forty years he is schooled in the hardest school of all. After eighty years of preparations and instruction and spiritual education, that man is brought out as the one who is going to be used to be instrumental in forming the people of God.

I want you to note that God's ways are always the same. This may bring comfort to you; it may bring discomfort to you, I do not know. If we have any burden for the people of God or for the interests of God, then we can be absolutely sure that God will take hold of us. He will apprehend us on the ground of the basis of this principle. He will lead us into ways to do things with us that may seem very, very strange to us indeed. But the whole end in view is a people–the reproduction of a people. It will be a very blessed thing if you were to take Abraham, Isaac, Jacob, Joseph and Moses and see if you could find that principle in those five lives. I think you would be very blessed if you just did a simple study on that line and you would learn a lot from it.

Note that the opening phrase of Exodus says, "Now these are the names of the sons of Israel," but in Hebrew it is simply "And." "And these are the names of the sons of Israel who came into Egypt." Then at the end of the book of Exodus, you suddenly find that for the first time God's glory is discovered. For the first time, God's glory takes up its permanent abode. I do not know whether many of you have perhaps realised that the first time that the glory of the Lord is ever actually mentioned is in the book of Exodus. In the whole book of Genesis you will not find the glory of the Lord. Isn't that instructive? You will not find the glory of the Lord in the whole book of Genesis. The word is not mentioned.

Where do you find glory? You find glory in Exodus. You find glory touching the earth in Exodus. Now that is wonderful—the glory of the Lord touching the earth. Furthermore you find the glory of the Lord taking up its abode on the earth. It is not just touching the top of Mount Sinai, not just causing great earthquakes and thunder and lightning and fire and so on, but actually taking up its abode at the heart of the people of God. Isn't that wonderful? The first time you find the glory of the Lord mentioned, is in the book of Exodus. There you already have a clue to a wonderful discovery about the Lord. The glory of the Lord is linked with the corporate. Never forget that. The glory of the Lord is linked with the corporate, and it can never touch anything that has not been redeemed. So we now find ourselves in this book. At the beginning of Exodus, we find, "And these are the names ..." At the end of the book we find a house filled with God's glory.

The Authorship of Exodus

Now, what about the authorship of Exodus? I do not think we have any difficulty here, in general. Exodus was not edited. Genesis was edited. It was compiled and edited. Exodus was written by Moses, therefore, Moses is the author of Exodus, and as I see it, the editor of Genesis. If you want to have some proof for Moses' authorship, then you will find it three times mentioned in this book. In Exodus 17:14, in Exodus 24:4, and in Exodus 34:27. In those three, you will find something mentioned of Moses writing this down. It says for instance in Exodus in 24:4, "Moses wrote all the words of the Lord, and rose up early in the morning." It would seem from these different references that this part of the Pentateuch was written by Moses after the actual events happened. In other words, it is probable that the account we have here was written very swiftly after these things happened. It is not at the very end of his life that he wrote it. I won't go into it now, but there are some very, very interesting clues to that. It is interesting, if any of you would like to follow it up.

It is very, very interesting to find that Exodus bears the atmosphere about it of an eyewitness account. I do not know if you have noticed that, but it has an atmosphere of an eyewitness. This is often the kind of clue as to when something was written. You do not find it a dry history written in a very difficult way. All kinds of small things seem to have been jotted down just after they happened.

Another interesting thing, as someone has pointed out is that if anyone else had written Exodus, they would never have spoken about Moses in the way that Moses is spoken about in this part of the Pentateuch. You know someone did in the end, write a little bit at the very, very end of Deuteronomy and they spoke of Moses as one of the greatest heroes of the people of God. But the impressive thing is that throughout Exodus, Moses is very much kept in the background.

For instance, we are told that Moses could not speak. Moses did not want to go to the people of God. He almost had to be dragged along. He said he couldn't talk, he did not have the gift of speech, he was slow of tongue. He said, "Why didn't the Lord find someone else?" Then when the Lord said, "Well, I'm going to send you," he said, "Well ... well ... bless the man you're going to send, Lord." In other words, Moses was saying, "I'm not going. You bless the man you're going to send, Lord." The Lord got rather angry with him then, and said that he was to take Aaron his brother and Aaron would do all the talking. The fact is that Aaron never did much talking in the life of Moses. But it is interesting to note that all Moses' weaknesses are given their right place in this record. People have pointed out that anyone else writing this story would have been very careful to have given a very, very much more, shall we say, happy account of Moses himself and the role that he played.

Have you ever noticed for instance that in this book, Moses hardly attributes anything to himself. At all the different points through it, he makes out that it was others. For instance, when judges were appointed, it is clearly pointed out that it was Jethro who suggested it, not Moses. On the question of priesthood and other things, it is pointed out that Aaron was the source of this and not Moses. Right the way through Exodus, you find that it was other people who were the source of different things, and not Moses. It is very interesting, but I think we will have to leave that.

The Date of the Writing

The date of Exodus would seem to be approximately 1400 years before Christ. Another very interesting point is that Exodus covers 81 years. I trust that this point will be instructive. The first 12 chapters cover 80 years, and from chapter 13 right through to chapter 40, covers under a year. Actually all of Leviticus, and quite a portion of Numbers too, make up the year. Isn't it interesting? Eighty years in a few chapters, and under a few months, perhaps two thirds of the year in a large number of chapters. What is the Lord teaching us in this? Well, you know, a tremendous amount of history, for the most part humdrum, routine, hidden history, insignificant to us and to men, has to be made for God to really act swiftly. It has been said that it was this one year, from which the whole of Jewish history springs. All Jewish law, the foundation of Jewish spiritual life, and everything to do with Jewish theology springs out of this one year. It centres in Mount Sinai. It centres in the giving of the Law and the showing of the tabernacle. That was all one year, but eighty years lay behind that one year and it is very instructive to us all.

Exodus 1-12	= 80 years
Exodus 13-40, + Leviticus + part of Numbers	= less than one year

I think some of us want to see the Lord move very fast, but you know, sometimes, the Lord has a long, painful, humdrum, routine history that lies behind some of His quickest movements.

When you think of the Lord Jesus' three years' ministry that shattered the world and has shattered it ever since—three years in which He did the work of God, the work of the ages, three years in which He accomplished the salvation of the whole of humanity from Adam to the last man that is to be born, and yet, behind it were thirty years of hidden, routine history in His own home and in His carpenter shop. The same is true of John the Baptist. Some rank John the Baptist amongst the eight greatest men that the world has ever produced. Yet, do you know how long John the Baptist's public ministry lasted? Six months. His ministry, the duration of his ministry, was six months. He also had thirty years' hidden history in the desert. So let's take courage from these things, that behind God's greatest movements are long hidden histories. Here we have it in this book of Exodus.

The Key to Exodus

What is the key to the book? It is a two-fold key. It is simply redemption and the house of God. These two sides can never be divorced. I think that one of the tragic things that Christendom has suffered from more than anything else was that at the Reformation they divorced redemption from the house of God. We have suffered from this ever since the Reformation. One of our greatest scholars, Professor F.F. Bruce, has said recently that since the Reformation, there has never been a satisfactory doctrine of the church set forth by any part of the church of God. There was such a reaction against Rome at the Reformation, that when they came out, everything was personal, and everything was individual. Consequently, redemption and salvation were divorced from the corporate, and a very real stress has been laid upon personal salvation, personal sanctification, and personal glorification, going on with the Lord personally. That is all very right, very good, very true, but the book of Exodus deals with the question of redemption.

The Theme of Exodus

You remember what the Bible is, don't you? It is not just a collection of writings about God; it is a definite, progressive revelation. In Genesis we find the beginnings of everything. We find God there in election; He is purposing something. Exodus reveals to us the redemption of God. It is the foundation in the Bible for all teaching about redemption. It all goes back to this book of Exodus: redemption. But you find that redemption has another side and you cannot divorce that side from it. Indeed, when I was studying this through these last few days, I seriously wondered whether to drop redemption out of it altogether, as far as the key to this book goes. Because you will find the word redemption about three, or at the most four times in the whole, whereas in Leviticus, you find it again and again and again and again! It is most interesting–what you do find in this book is a people, a people, a people, a people, all of the time it is a people. Nevertheless, redemption's there, but the other side of redemption is a people. You cannot divorce these two sides, one is the means, the other is the end. The means is redemption, the end is the house of God. God's redemptive purpose is to have a dwelling place. God's redeeming work is to produce a people, you see? If we are just redeemed and we stay there, we miss the point of our redemption! There are two sides to it: God redeems us as a means to an end. He redeems us to plant us in the land, to have us as a dwelling place. God's glory is bound up with that dwelling place. So, wherever we turn in the book of Exodus, we find this two-fold theme.

At the beginning we have deliverance. What is it? It is the deliverance of a people. If you look at the end, we have the house of God and God dwelling in it. At the beginning we have redemption by a lamb, a perfect lamb without spot, without blemish being sacrificed, a people taken out of Egypt, a people delivered. At the end we have God's glory filling His dwelling place in the midst of His redeemed people. So, on one side we have a people delivered, a nation born, on the other side, we have something shown, a pattern of something shown, which is the embodiment of all that God desires for that redeemed people. We do not believe that all the redeemed will be part of that house. But we believe that God's goal is to make all the redeemed part of that house. His goal is to have everyone part of that house, built together as living stones. He has made provision for every redeemed child of His to become part of that dwelling place. That is God's end, and redemption is the means to it.

Remember what the key was to Genesis? Beginning. The beginning of everything. The key to Exodus is redemption and the house of God. In other words, we have now come out of the beginnings of all and have got down to the bedrock of it again.

Exodus is divided into three parts: the first is to do with the deliverance from Egypt, the second is the covenant of Sinai, and the third is the house of God revealed and built. The first is a people delivered, and the second is a people in covenant relationship. That is very important. A people delivered is one thing and a people in covenant relationship is another. The last is a people built together as God's dwelling place.

A People Delivered

The Preparation of Moses

Now in the first portion of Exodus, you will find that it deals with the preparation of Moses in the first four chapters. You will remember what a wonderful story that is. I think Exodus is as thrilling, if not more thrilling than Genesis in its typology. I do not know if you have noticed that. Exodus is really wonderful in the way that it takes up different things and how they are to be taken up in the New Testament as speaking of the Lord Jesus, and of many other things. You remember how we are told these things happened as our examples.

Moses was prepared in those first four chapters. You find his prenatal history, and you find also the history of his birth. Then you find the history of his education and the history of his walk with God. It is a very wonderful story. The most wonderful part of all was when God spoke with Moses.

Moses must have been a man of unusual courage. I was reading the Talmud the other day, not that you can think upon the Talmud as being inspired, but it said that Moses was a courageous man because he grazed his father-in-law's flock onto Mount Sinai, which no other shepherd had ever dared to do in history. It was always believed, even by the pagan people round about that God lived there on Mount Sinai. The grass was very beautiful and not eaten by flocks and Moses saw this and he grazed his flocks. Incidentally I do not know if this was a disregard for divinity or deity or what it was that he grazed his father-in-law's flock on the face of Mount Sinai. It was there that he saw the bush as if on fire, and yet was not consumed. There is something very wonderful about poor Moses. You will remember that Moses was a very different man to the man at the beginning.

The Judgments Upon Egypt

Secondly, you will find that the next chapters (5–12), deal with the judgments of God upon Egypt. We forget, you know, that for any man or woman who has been redeemed it meant tremendous judgment upon satanic authority. I do not believe that we as the children of God realise what it means spiritually. It is only when we see souls endeavouring to come to the Lord and in the grip of something far, far more powerful than they can do anything about that we realise what a major thing it is to be redeemed. I do not know whether that has spoken anything to your hearts, but I have seen in my short experience, souls get through something that holds onto them with an iron-like grasp and will not let them go. Well, that is Egypt.

You must not think that the enemy is just a little bit weak on you and because of that you escaped and somehow came to the Lord. Many people's idea of coming to the Lord is that you make a decision at some point and it is just as easy as that. Believe me, the shocking things that took place behind the scenes at Calvary, the satanic devices, have been the means of our redemption. On one side you have the joy of deliverance. On the other side you have the most terrible judgment. That is the explanation for many of the Lord's sayings, for instance, "Now the prince of this world is cast out." We must remember there was tremendous judgment involved. (Since this is only a bird's eye view of Exodus, we cannot stay with this. However, there is in Exodus an amazing study just within the ten plagues.)

The Passover

Then you remember the plagues end with the Passover. The blood of the lamb was put upon the doorposts and the lintels and the Angel of Death passed over—the institution of the Passover. In chapter 13–15 they have the Exodus. The people are released, the people move out from Egypt, the people are pursued, and the people miraculously are delivered at the shore of the Red Sea. Then the Egyptian host is destroyed in the sea. So, that is the first part in this deliverance.

You know it is not fanciful to see in here (as the New Testament narrative sees) the most wonderful foreshadowing of the Lord Jesus. It is the most remarkable thing. You remember, even in His birth the edict talked about the male children at that time. It bears such a resemblance to this famous story—the Lord's remarkable preservation, His hidden history, and then after that the terrible judgment at Calvary upon Satan.

The Lord Himself, speaking in Luke's Gospel about "when My exodus is upon you.[1]" He looked upon Calvary as an exodus. It was the deliverance of a people. As I have already mentioned to you, this is the principle of the whole book: God always begins with one and produces a people. The Lord Jesus is God's great progenitor of the people of God. It began with one and ends with a people.

---

1 See Luke 9:31 the same word as Exodus is used for either 'departure' or 'decease' in different versions

That is why the Lord Jesus spoke of a grain of wheat falling into the ground and dying.

So, the deliverance is a very, very wonderful thing. It involves a deep hidden separation. It involves a terrible judgment. It involves the death of an innocent life. It involves the deliverance of a people.

A People in Covenant Relationship

When we come to the next part of Exodus, you will find the journey from the Red Sea to Sinai. This section is filled with instruction. For instance, when I think of the pool of Marah and what it means (see Exodus 15:22–25a). If I may just say, I have often thought of how remarkable it is that the Lord should put into such small instances so much spiritual value. You know, many of our lives are just like the pools of Marah. They are bitter. We know they are bitter and others know they are bitter. No one can drink of it. They are brackish. There may be all kinds of things that have done that to our lives, but there you are, they are like the pools of Marah. They look very nice; they look very inviting, but they are bitter. When people drink from the waters in our lives they find they are not what they look like. You know that beside the pool of Marah stood a tree. Trees in scripture always speak of paths of life … and it seems to me that Marah with the tree at its side speaks of a life that has not yet repudiated its failure. Because of that, it is not life giving. But Moses was told to cut the tree down and toss it into the water and the waters then became sweet.

These small, small incidents are placed there for spiritual value. We have to learn that sometimes because our lives are brackish and the waters of our lives are bitter, there is only one way out that is positive. It is the repudiation of our failure. Something is thrown into the water and let go of there, and then the waters are healed.

Giving the Law

When you turn to chapter 20, you find the beginning of the law. Why did the Lord speak so much about this? Why are these few chapters from 20–23 the foundation for so much later on? This is the whole dispensation called the dispensation of law. Paul, referring to it, speaks of it as Mount Sinai. He speaks of one whole age, one whole dispensation as being Mount Sinai. He speaks of two dispensations: Mount Sinai and the other Zion, these two different ages. Here you have Sinai and all that Sinai stands for. I want you to note how remarkable these chapters are. Perhaps you will be ever so amazed at the way the Lord comes right down to the most practical details about people's land and whether, if you lend money to the poor, you should take interest. If you take a person's clothes as they did in the East as a pledge for lending them money you should return it that night lest they die of the cold. You will find them all here. The Lord took Moses up to the top of Sinai to tell him all these things.

However, you see here you have what we call a moral righteousness. First of all we have the ten commandments, as I trust you all know, and out of the ten commandments we have the expansion of the ten commandments (Exodus 21–23). The question of not making any graven images is expanded and our whole relationship to God is brought into view. First, the Sabbath is brought into view. This whole question of first fruits is brought into view. Then our relationship to the Lord and then our relationship to our husbands and wives is brought into view, followed by our relationship to our children, then our relationship to slaves, then our relationship to the government and to aliens in our land. Everything is covered by this law that is given. That is the law. He brings it right down to practical terms. Sometimes I wonder if the Lord's people have taken the law, in a right way, to their heart. I could say a little bit more about that in a moment. I want to leave it like that for now.

The Ratification of the Covenant

God gives the law and when He has given the law, Moses comes down the mount to the people and he reads what is called "The Book of the Law." Exodus 20–23 is called the book of the law. He reads it to them and the people said, "All that the Lord has spoken we will do." Moses slayed the bullock and the blood is sprinkled upon the book and upon the people and the people again say, "All that the Lord has told you we will do, and be obedient."

This is the ratification of God's covenant. God has now taken a further step. First, He delivered a people, now He puts Himself into covenant relationship with the people. He says to the people, "Here is the basis of My covenant" and the people say, "Lord, if that is the basis of Your covenant, we will do it. We will be obedient." Moses tells them to get an ox and slay it. Then he sprinkles the book and sprinkles the people.

What does this speak of? It speaks simply that God is making a covenant with His people on the grounds of no unrighteousness. He said, my basis for doing this is that someone has died for you, and in him you have died. In other words, even under the old covenant there was something of the shedding of blood and of death. It meant that there are two sides of death. Someone died for the people and the people died in that someone. God made a covenant and from that day we find a people in a covenant relationship with the Lord. From that day, the Jew boasted wherever he went that he belonged to the covenant people of God. God has made a covenant with him. God said, "I will make you My peculiar treasure among the nations of the earth." Ever afterwards the prophets always spoke of this covenant as a marriage covenant—God bringing a people into a marriage relationship with Himself and making a covenant with them. Well, that is really the second portion of Exodus.

The House of God Revealed

The last portion of Exodus is from chapters 25–40. In that portion the one thing that is talked about is the tabernacle. Some people do not like us repeating things, but it is a very interesting thing how the Bible repeats itself. I do not know if any of you have been wrung at all by Exodus because first of all you get the law given in one place and in the next three chapters it repeats it all over again. Then you get the building of the tabernacle and then it all repeats it all over again after one chapter is done. I think the Lord sometimes has to do that kind of thing for various reasons not only to really emphasise and to write it upon our hearts but also to make things utterly clear.

The Pattern Given

You will see that the explanation in Exodus 25–31 is the pattern revealed. God takes Moses up again into the mount. Now this is interesting. First of all Moses has gone up into the mountain and the law was given to him. Then he went down from the mount and the law was ratified amongst the people. Then God spoke to him again and he goes up again into Sinai, into the cloud. For forty days and forty nights he was away from the view of the people. I think most of you will know what happened in that forty days and forty nights. (I might just say that it is very, very interesting how the theme of forty occurs again and again in the book of Exodus.) You will find that whilst he was up there forty days and forty nights, God showed to him the pattern. Many people have wrongly understood this word "pattern." They think it is a blueprint. I have often heard people speak about God showing Moses the blueprint of the tabernacle. But the word does not mean that at all. It means the type, or He showed Him the type itself. He saw something up there. It was not just a blueprint; he looked on something. He saw something, and he came down with something clearly in his mind and heart.

Failure or Faithfulness

You will notice then a terrible thing as we are beginning to work through the Word of God. It is true in every new movement of God. Moses comes down and for the first time in the history of the human race God has disclosed fully His heart's desire. And as Moses comes down (you know the Lord told Moses to go down) as he comes down he finds the whole camp in a riot. A golden calf has been made and the people are drinking and eating and playing. Aaron himself has fashioned the calf. He made it. You know the story. Moses broke the tablets of stone and ground the calf into the water and made the people drink it. The most serious and the most terrible, solemn side of it all was when Moses said, "Whoever is on the Lord's side, let him come unto me" and the whole house of Levi came to Moses. Moses said, "Take your swords and go throughout the whole camp from end to end. Let every man slay his brother and his father, slay his closest relative. You must go through the camp and put an end to this terrible thing" and it says that the sons of Levi did as Moses commanded them.

The Covenant Renewed

Then you find a remarkable thing. God called Moses again up into the mount and renewed the covenant. No sooner had the covenant been made, than the people broke it and as soon as the people broke it, God renewed it. But you will note an interesting thing. In chapter 33–34, God reiterates all that He had said in the earlier chapters 20–23, with some significant differences. He leaves out everything to do with our relationship with one another. In the renewing of the covenant He only sketches the relationship with Himself. Isn't that interesting? Because obviously, what had happened to Israel was that they forgot their relationship to the Lord although their relationship with one another still held good. The Lord was stressing once again the need of a direct personal relationship with Himself.

Building the House of God

Then the last chapters are to do with the building of the house, not the revealing of it, but the actual building of the house. There is another interesting thing that I might just point out: the Lord gives the pattern of the house and there is immediate failure. Just as with Adam: there was failure. Noah: there was a failure. Shem: there was a failure. Even when Abraham was in the land, he went down to Egypt. All is failure. When it comes here to the covenant made with the people, there is immediate failure. The interesting thing is that the Levites come into view. This has a great spiritual lesson for us: because of man, things are always failing, but God always has His spiritual "Levites." He always has that which would give Him His right. God is prepared to go on with what will give Him His right. So, He renewed the covenant on the grounds of men that are so utter that they are prepared to slay even their own sons and fathers, their own relatives.

That is a very hard-hitting thing isn't it? When we see this whole question of the church, our affections and our desires and the things that are closest to us, they are the things that hinder us. The Levites were those that were so wholly with God that as much as they loved those closest and nearest to them, they had to take the sword sometimes to the closest and most intimate ties, because and for the sake of the Lord.

The Message of Exodus

Thus we find the book of Exodus in outline. The whole book from end to end has its three parts and the foundation of it all is simply this question of redemption. What is the message of this book? What is the message of this part of the Pentateuch? It is simply that God has redeemed us with a tremendous goal in view. That is really the message of the book: God has redeemed us with a tremendous goal in view. If we stop short at the means we shall never reach the end. We must look upon our redemption, our salvation as a means, and not as an end. When we come to the Lord we have got to recognise that the goal is ahead. Our salvation is not the goal. Our salvation is but the means to an end. We have also got to recognise that nothing short of that goal will ever satisfy God and nothing short of that goal will ever inherit the glory of God. Those two things go together. Our redemption is a means to an end.

If we sum it all up, we see four things in the book of Exodus. The first is that God reveals Himself for the first time in history by His name Jehovah. I AM that I AM—the name that always speaks of God's redeeming love for us. He reveals Himself for the first time as Jehovah and ever after we find that name always brings into view, God's covenant, God's grace, and God's redemption.

The second thing we find about this book is that it is the realisation of our redemption. God has the Lamb slain from the foundation of the world and by that Lamb He has made realised our redemption. Our redemption is legal in its foundation in the sense that someone has died for us and therefore, as it were, the Angel of death has passed us over. We have been wonderfully, legally saved. But secondly, there is practical salvation, because God has not only legally saved us from the world, from sin, and from death, but He has wonderfully delivered us out of this present evil age. We have this two-fold redemption, which is very,

very wonderful. On one side we have the Lamb slain for us; on the other side we have a wonderful deliverance from this present age and kingdom.

The Basis for our Redemption

Then you will also notice that there is a basis for our redemption. I do not think many of us sufficiently understand this. Many people have the idea that because God is very merciful He just pats us on the back and says, "I'm terribly sorry about the mess you have got yourself into, but don't worry. I will save you." Many peoples' idea of the cross is just that. It is God becoming all loving. He sort of looks at the whole humanity and says, "I'm so sorry about all of this. I will save you."

The basis of our redemption is a fulfilled law. It is the ten commandments and the whole expansion of the law utterly kept! Perfect righteousness is the basis of redemption. Perfected moral righteousness is the basis of redemption. No one has ever been saved apart from a perfected righteousness. Every man and every woman that has ever been saved has been saved on the basis of a law that has been utterly kept.

The Fulfilment of the Law

You know what that means. It means that Christ is the end of the law or the fulfilment of the law to everyone that believes. God could never have saved you or me if there had not been One who was perfected moral righteousness. It sounds very technical, but the Lord Jesus is perfected moral righteousness. Everything you find in Deuteronomy, everything you find in Numbers, everything you find in Leviticus, everything you find in Exodus about the law, the Lord Jesus kept perfectly. He was perfect moral righteousness—God-ward, man-ward, self-ward. He kept the law in every single part. On that ground God saved you and saved me. But does that mean that you and I can do anything? Surely not. For the one who kept the law perfectly in every point, although tested in all points like as we are, is inside and the law of the Spirit of life is now the thing that will govern.

This is the point: if you and I are walking according to the Spirit we shall find that the law of Exodus is kept. We will not be conscious of it. I have often noted that kind of thing. With some Christians it can truly be very hard to strike a bargain, and yet they think that they are walking fully in the Spirit. Some Christians can lend and expect a very big interest on what they lend a brother or a sister. You see if we live according to the Spirit these are the things which should be checked up on. We may not be even conscious that they are in the Bible. But we should be conscious of something inside making us very uncomfortable about this. Later on as we read we shall find, "Oh, I never did realise that."

I remember the shock (I will say I so failed on this point); I remember the shock I once had when I was responsible for someone's wages but I kept them overnight. I never really thought about it, but I remember there came a point where I became very uncomfortable and I could not think why. Until over the weekend I happened to be reading a passage of the New Testament something that just simply said, "Thou shalt not keep the wages of him overnight." You see even in the small things to do with our lives we may all fail in many points and we do fail. But if we walk according to the Spirit we shall find that the Lord is going to, by the law of the Spirit of life inside, work out something. Let us note that.

Let us also note that the end of our redemption is the house of God and the land. The Lord saved us, He redeemed us on the basis that the Lord Jesus has kept the law. But you know it is all so wonderfully true that the end of our redemption is the house of God. To be really built in to the house of God. That is the end of our redemption, and not only to be built in to the house of God but also to be in the land. The house of God speaks of God's dwelling place, the land always speaks of the fullness of Christ. So, remember that the end of our redemption is to become part of God's dwelling place and the end of becoming part of God's dwelling place is to become those that become the fullness of Him that filleth all in all. You and I are destined to become the fullness of Him that filleth all in all.

Lord, we do ask Thee to just take these words and blot out anything untoward, anything Lord, that is not of Thyself. But then write upon our hearts and in our spirits, Lord, everything that is of Thyself that we may learn thereby. Lord, we do pray that the goal and the end of our redemption shall be wonderfully and gloriously achieved by Thy grace. We shall become those, Lord, who become Thy dwelling place. A home of God. A habitation of God in the Spirit. We ask it in His precious name and for His sake. Amen.

9.
Exodus
Study Guide

The Hebrew title is "these are the names of," taken from the opening phrase of the book in Hebrew. Exodus comes from the Greek and means "departure" or "going out"—the same word as is used in Luke 9:31, II Peter 1:15.

In Genesis, all God's workings were towards a people. From the beginning of Exodus we have a people. Note carefully the opening verse of Exodus 1. "These are the names ... who came into Egypt" v1 "... seventy souls" v5, "and the children of Israel were fruitful ... multiplied ... and the land was filled with them" v7. The Exodus was the departure from Egypt of this divinely redeemed and constituted people. It is interesting to note that the book ends with a description of "The glory of the Lord" in relation to this people, the first time in the Bible that we find the glory of God touching the Earth.

Authorship and Date

Exodus is the work of Moses—compare Exodus 17:14, 24:4, 34:27. He, at any rate, appears to have been the human instrument. In fact the history of Israel as a nation really begins with Moses. In later years, Israel looked back on the deliverance from Egypt, and the covenant at Sinai, as the basic events of the national history, and Moses as the supreme architect, humanly speaking, of the nation.

The book was written in the wilderness period about 1400 BC and covers a duration of 81 years.

Exodus 1–12 = 80 years

Exodus 12–40 = 1 year

Key to the Book

The key is a threefold one—Redemption, the Word of God and the House of God, and these three matters can never be divorced. The former two are the means and the latter is the end. Wherever we turn in this book we find this threefold theme. At the beginning we find a people delivered and born, who are to live by the Word of God. At the end we find the Tabernacle, which represents the desire of God for His redeemed People. This should be a means of great instruction to us, for our redemption is the means by which God saves and delivers us, and His Word is the means by which He forms and sustains us, both with the goal that we might become His dwelling place. Do we, in fact, ever find in the Bible redemption without the House of God in view?

Outline of the Book

In this book, we have three main events recorded. We have the redemption and deliverance of Israel (Passover and Exodus); the constitution of Israel at Sinai as the elect nation, through whom "the seed of the woman" (Genesis 3:5) should ultimately come—the revelation of His eternal Purpose (the tabernacle representing the dwelling place of God)

Message of the Book

The message is that God has redeemed us with a tremendous goal in view. Nothing short of it can satisfy God, or inherit His glory.

In Exodus 6:6–8, God promises: "I will bring you out ... I will bring you in"; out of the house of bondage into the House of God; out of the land of Egypt into the land of promise—out of self and into Christ.

Thus, we see in Exodus:

I. The Revelation

of God's Redeeming name, Jehovah (Exodus 3)

II. The Realisation

and Basis of our Redemption (Exodus 5–24).

The judgment of Egypt, the Passover, the Exodus. A people redeemed and delivered.

III. The Fulfilled Law

perfect righteousness, found only in Christ.

IV. The End

of our Redemption—Exodus 25–40. The house of God and the promised land.

Summary of Contents

I. The Deliverance

from Egypt (Exodus 1:1–15:21)

    A. The Condition of the Israelites (chapters 1–2)

        1. Slaves of Pharaoh (xviii Dynasty, Thothmes I) (Exodus 1)

        2. The cry for deliverance (Exodus 2)

    B. The preparation of the deliverer, Moses (meaning "drawn out") (Exodus 2–4)

        1. The natural preparation (40 years) (Exodus 2:1–15)

        2. The spiritual preparation (40 years) (Exodus 2:16–22)

        3. Revelation of Yahweh and commission (Exodus 3–4)

    C. The conflict with Egypt (Exodus 5–13)

        1. The command and promise of Yahweh (Exodus 5:1–7:7)

        2. The power of Yahweh—ten plagues (Exodus 7:8–12:36)

        3. The provision of Yahweh—the Passover Lamb (Exodus 12:37–13)

    D. The victory over Egypt (Exodus 14–15:21)

        1. The crossing of the Red Sea (Exodus 14)

        2. Song of deliverance led by Miriam (Exodus 15:1–21)

II. The Covenant at Sinai

(Exodus 15:22–24:18)

    A. In the Wilderness of Shur (Exodus 15:22–24)

        1. Marah–bitter water (Exodus 15:22–27)

        2. Elim—12 springs and 70 palm trees (Exodus 15:27)

    B. In the wilderness of sin (Exodus 16:1–12)

        1. Murmuring—no bread (Exodus 16:1–12)

        2. Quails and manna (Exodus 16:13–36)

    C. Rephidim (Exodus 17–18)

        1. Murmuring—no water—the smitten rock (Exodus 17:1–7)

        2. Amalek—victory of Joshua (Exodus 17:8–16

        3. The visit of Jethro (Exodus 18)

    D. In the Wilderness of Sinai (Exodus 19–24)

        1. The covenant (Exodus 19)

        2. The ten commandments (Exodus 20)

        3. The book of the covenant (Exodus 21–23)

        4. The ratification of the covenant (Exodus 24) (Hebrews 9:18–20)

III. The House of God

Revealed and Built

(Exodus 25:1–40)

    A. "Let them make Me a sanctuary" (Exodus 25:8; 25–27)

        1. The furniture, the hangings, and the boards of the tabernacle (Exodus 25–26)

        2. The outer court (Exodus 27)

    B. Priesthood (Exodus 28–31)

1. Their garments—the high priest and priests (Exodus 28–30)

2. Their consecration—"That they minister unto Me" (Exodus 29)

3. Their ministry of intercession—altar of incense (Exodus 30)

4. Their ministry of life and holiness—laver

C. Workmen–chosen and equipped (Exodus 31)

D. The Failure of the people (Exodus 32–34)

1. Golden Calf; "Who is on the Lord's side?" the tribe of Levi (Exodus 32)

2. Moses' intercession on the mount (Exodus 33–34)

E. The tabernacle "According to the Pattern" (Exodus 25:40; 35–40

1. The hangings, boards, furniture and outer court (Exodus 35–38)

2. The priests' garments (Exodus 39)

F. "The glory of the Lord filled the tabernacle" (Exodus 40)

Recommended Books:

The Exodus and the Wanderings in the Wilderness
(Bible History Vol. 2)
   A. Edersheim
Notes on Exodus
   C.H. MacIntosh
An Outline of Exodus
   C.A. Coates
Christ in the Tabernacle
   A.B. Simpson
God's Dwelling Place
   Bakht Singh

Questions

1. What are the key words in the book of Exodus?

2. Why are they three fold?

3. What New Testament Gospel does Exodus correlate with and why?

4. Draw a timeline of the journeying of the Israelites? Is there any significance in the places the Lord stops them?

5. What is the significance of each of the Ten Commandments in the light of Christ?

6. Explain the significance of the altar and the laver?

7. What do the fabrics and their colours used in the priestly garments signify?

8. Choose two other servants of God in Scripture who had natural preparation followed by spiritual preparation. What can we learn in comparing these men to Moses?

9. What do you learn about God from the following passages:
a) Exodus 5:3, 6:2–4

b) Exodus 15:22–27

c) Exodus 25:8

d) Exodus 25:40

10. Using the Book of Exodus sum up God's eternal purpose?

10.
Leviticus
Study Guide

Introduction

When we come to this book, we find that God has taken another step forward. In Exodus, we see Him saving and delivering a people, and establishing among them His dwelling place. In Leviticus, He speaks from within that dwelling place, in the midst of the people. God has, for the first time, taken up residence amongst a people. The problem, which the book of Leviticus deals with, is how a failing redeemed people may dwell in the presence of a Holy God, without being destroyed; how indeed they might fulfil His purpose for them to be His home.

Technically, this book contains the order for priestly and Levitical service in all of its aspects. The tribe of Levi was set apart for the service of God, in lieu of all the first born sons of Israel, and came to be known as "the Levites." One family in particular, that of Aaron, was set apart as priests. Once understood, the book of Leviticus becomes one of the most helpful books in the Bible, dealing, as it does, with the basis for the service, worship and testimony of the people of God; the basis for their acceptance and continued standing before Him; what is in "the way of Holiness."

Authorship and Date

We are not told about the writing down of the laws contained in this book, but it is repeatedly stated that the laws were given through Moses. The phrase, "the Lord spoke unto Moses" is used about 30 times, and 20 of the 27 chapters begin that way. Verses such as Exodus 24:7 entitle us to suppose that either Moses wrote these laws, or that he personally supervised the writing of them.

Leviticus would have been written during the stay at the foot of Mt. Sinai (see Leviticus 18:3), and was written after the erection of the Tabernacle (Leviticus 1:1).

Key to the Book

The key is bound up with these phrases: "I am the Lord thy God" (21 times), "before the Lord" (60 times approx), "Unto the Lord" (80 times approx), and the opening phrase: "And the Lord called" (Leviticus 1:1).

The key is the standing of the people of God before Him. Firstly, the basis upon which He can call them to be His people, to become partakers of the divine nature, to be His dwelling place—the basis upon which He can continue with them. Secondly, it addresses the basis of their relationship to Him, their service unto Him, and their acceptance, etc.

Outline of the Book

The heart of the whole book is chapter 16, "the day of atonements". This gathers up all else, from beginning to end, in itself, the one great annual atonement for all the sins of the whole people.

We find a threefold division in this book:

I. Sacrifice (Leviticus 1:1–6:7)

II. Meditation (Leviticus 6:8–10)

III. Sanctification (Leviticus 11–27)

    A. Separation from all uncleanness (Leviticus 11–15)

    B. The rights of the Lord—positive holiness (Leviticus 17–27)

I. Sacrifice

A. Note first the order. It is quite different to what works out in practice. The burnt offering precedes the others in revelation, although, in actual fact, we come to God first as trespassers and sinners.

B. The burnt offering, the meal offering and the peace offering are linked together.

    1. The burnt offering:

Christ our substitute and representative—dying in our place for
what we should have done—the will of God from the heart.
The Lord wants all, not part; the fire on the altar consumes
everything, reducing it to ashes. See Romans 12:1–2.

    2. The meal offering:

Christ our substitute and representative—dying in
our place for what we should have been—sinless"
True, perfect, humanity. No leaven, no honey, always salt. Flour,
oil, frankincense—priests to eat part of this. See Ephesians 4.

3. The peace offering:

Christ our substitute and representative—dying in our place for what we should have known—peace with God and unity with all His people.

Worship, oneness, and fellowship—all take part. See Ephesians 2:13–22 and compare 1 Corinthians 12 with Romans 1–16

A. The sin offering and the trespass offering are linked together.

1. The sin offering:

Christ our substitute for what we have been by nature and practice—sinners. Sins of commission—this includes all sin knowingly committed.

2. The trespass offering:

Christ our substitute for what we have not done, thus sinning against God and man. Sins of omission—this includes all sin unconsciously committed.

II. Mediation

Note the importance of the priest's function (garments, anointing, salt). He symbolises service. Notice also that the Lord Jesus is the Mediator, our High Priest, and fulfils the type. Nevertheless, we also as His people, under Him and with Him are all priests unto God. See Hebrews 9:11–15, 1 Peter 2:4–5

III. Sanctification

We come now to practical sanctification. Leviticus 11:44–45; cf. 15:31

A. Firstly, separation from all uncleanness. It deals with food, clean and unclean. There is a need for discrimination and circumspection. It also deals with the natural birth and forbidden relationships for marriage. This speaks of the need for the cross to deal with all aspects of our natural life—natural affections and relationships etc. The cross must deal with all our links to the old creation. Provision is also made for leprosy—symbolic of sin—in persons, garments, and houses.

B. Secondly, the rights of the Lord—positive holiness. How often we meet the phrase "I am the Lord". Everything is linked with our relationship to Him.

C. We see also in the sabbatical system, the seventh day, the seventh week, the seventh month, the seventh year, seven weeks of years, the rest and sanctification of the Lord. In the year of Jubilee, we see everything returning, and there is restitution and liberation, the Land belonging to the Lord Himself. Leviticus 25:23

Message of the Book

We have been called to the dwelling place of God and God has made provision for us to be there.

The only way that God's dwelling place can be built is by way of the burnt offering, by clear separation, and by giving the Lord His rights. Nevertheless, we meet the problem of an old nature, of indwelling sin, of failure and error. For all this, the Lord has made wonderful provision in the death of the Lord Jesus. Thus, we find that Christ crucified for us and as us is the foundation of God's dwelling place, His eternal home, and all the spiritual building work in charge of the Holy Spirit in connection with it.

Note carefully that God always speaks with us from out of the Tent of Meeting. We must therefore bring all to the door.

Summary of Contents

I. Sacrifice (Leviticus 1–7)

A. The burnt offering (Leviticus 1; 6:8–13)

Without blemish, presented alive, slain before the Lord, laying on of hands, all consumed by fire

B. The meal offering (Leviticus 2:6:14–23)

Fine flour, oil and frankincense—no leaven—shared by priests—consumed by fire

C. The peace offering (Leviticus 3:7:11–18)

Without blemish—presented alive—laying on of hands—priests sprinkled with blood—fat burned—shared by offerer

D. The sin offering (Leviticus 4:1–5:13; 6:24–30)

Without blemish—blood sprinkled—fat burned on altar—carcass burned without the camp—atonement and forgiveness

E. The trespass offering (Leviticus 5:14–6:7; 7:1–7)

Without blemish—restitution, atonement and forgiveness

II. Mediation (Leviticus 8–10)

A. Leviticus 8: the consecration of the priests

Their cleansing, clothing, anointing, offerings, separation

B. Leviticus 9: the sacrifices of the high priest

Note this was the first time a high priest had offered sacrifices.

C. Leviticus 10: the failure of Nadab and Abihu; presumption and disobedience. Strange fire and terrible judgment

III. Sanctification

(Leviticus 11–27)

A. Separation from all uncleanness

    1. Leviticus 11: Clean Food:

clean and unclean animals

    2. Leviticus 12: Child Birth

    3. Leviticus: Leprosy

    4. Leviticus 14: The Leper's Offering

    5. Leviticus 15: Uncleanness

    6. Leviticus 16: Day of Atonement

B. The rights of the Lord

    1. Positive holiness

        a) Leviticus 17: sacrifices acceptable to

God; drinking of blood prohibited

        b) Leviticus 18: forbidden degrees of marriage

        c) Leviticus 19–20: laws and penalties default

        d) Leviticus 21–22: regulations

for priests and sacrifices

    2. The rest and satisfaction of the Lord

        a) Feasts of the Lord

- The Sabbath: 7th day (Leviticus 23:1–13) (remember the figure 7 speaks of fullness, or completeness)
- The Passover: 14th day of first month, (Leviticus 23:4–5)
- Unleavened Bread: 15th to 21st days of 1st month, (Leviticus 23:6–8)

- First Fruits: 16th day of 1st month, (chapter 23:9–14)
- Pentecost (weeks) 6th day of 3rd month, (chapter 23:15–22) nb. 7 weeks completed from offering of first fruits
- Trumpets: 1st day of 7th month, (chapter 23:23–25)
- Day of Atonement: 10th day of 7th month (chapter 23:26–32)
- Tabernacles: 15th to 21st days of 7th month, (chapter 23:33–44)

b) Oil for the lamps and the showbread (Leviticus 24:1–9)

c) Penalty for blasphemy (Leviticus 24:10–23)

d) The Sabbath 7th year and year of jubilee—50th year (Leviticus 25:1–55)

e) Blessings and curses (Leviticus 26:1–46)

f) Vows and offerings (Leviticus 27:1–34)

Recommended Books

Law of Offerings
  Andrew Jukes
Leviticus
  Andrew Bonar
Notes on Leviticus
  C.H. Mackintosh

Questions

1. What is the central chapter in the book of Leviticus?

2. What does the Day of Atonement, chapter 16, teach us about the work of Jesus Christ (see Hebrews 9:1–28)?

3. Write out a list of the passages which mention the door of the Tent of Meeting. What does this teach you about worshipping and serving the Lord?

4. Read Leviticus 17:10–14. What does this tell you about the death of Christ?

5. Chapters 13–14 deal with leprosy. Do you think this means anything spiritually for the people of God today?

6. What do we learn about God's attitude to those who consult spirits and mediums from Leviticus 19:31; 20:6, 27:7?

7. What are the feasts of the Lord, as mentioned in chapters 23–25? (Give references) How are these feasts fulfilled in the New Testament?

8. Write a paragraph stating how Aaron, in his duties, and also by the garments that he wears, shows us something about Jesus Christ.(Compare Hebrews 4:14–5:10; 7:20; 10:22)

9. What lessons can Christians learn from the strange fire mentioned in 10:1 and 27

10. How is God's attitude towards Israel shown in the following places:
a)Leviticus 10:3

b) Leviticus 20:24–26

c)Leviticus 22:31–33

d) Leviticus 25:38

11. Read the food laws in chapter 11. Can you find anything there that could instruct Christians about their spiritual food?

12. In chapters 18–21, we are given some lessons in morality and justice. Do you think that these are good standards? If so why? (Write a paragraph on this.)

11.
Numbers:
Responsibility

Numbers 1:1–3

And Jehovah spake unto Moses in the wilderness of Sinai, in the tent of meeting, on the first day of the second month, in the second year after they were come out of the land of Egypt, saying, Take ye the sum of all the congregation of the children of Israel, by their families, by their fathers' houses, according to the number of the names, every male, by their polls, from twenty years old and upward, all that are able to go forth to war in Israel, thou and Aaron shall number them by their hosts.

Numbers 26:1–2

And it came to pass after the plague, that Jehovah spake unto Moses and unto Eleazar the son of Aaron the priest, saying, Take the sum of all the congregation of the children of Israel, from twenty years old and upward, by their fathers' houses, all that are able to go forth to war in Israel.

Numbers 36:13

These are the commandments and the ordinances which Jehovah commanded by Moses unto the children of Israel in the plains of Moab by the Jordan at Jericho.

We have come now to the fourth part of the Pentateuch. You remember that we said at the very beginning that the Pentateuch is a five-fold volume, which is fundamental to the whole Word of God. Each part of this five-fold volume, each one of these five parts of this one volume has a distinct feature, and we have been looking together at each of them. In the book of Genesis we found in the beginning God was dealing with individuals on the whole and we find that it is a book of beginnings. That is the way that we can understand the first volume of the Pentateuch.

We say that the book of Exodus takes us a very big step forward. We find that God has a people, and that the opening verses of Exodus speak of the names. We find that this is a book of redemption, but we have found that redemption is not the substance of the book. Redemption, as we find in the book of Exodus, is the means to an end. The whole book moves toward the dwelling place of God. The heart is the dwelling place of God. In Genesis we find the beginning, the origin of it all. In Exodus we find the means to achieve it, the revelation of it, and we find the construction of it.

In Leviticus a very big step forward again has been taken. For the very first time, we find in the first chapter that God has taken up residence within His dwelling place in the midst of a people upon a fallen earth, and we find that He is speaking from out of the tent of meeting. Leviticus deals with the problem of how poor, failing, wayward children of God, such as we are, albeit redeemed, can be made the home of God. Leviticus deals with that problem alone. How can we, the redeemed, become part of the very home and habitation of God?

Themes in the Book of Numbers

When we first started on these studies, I remember saying to you that Numbers dealt with the aspect of conflict and pilgrimage. Pilgrimage and conflict. However, as I have looked at the book of Numbers, I have been deeply impressed, I am sure by the Holy Spirit that the main issue of this book is really the question of responsibility. We find that in this part of the Pentateuch, the whole ground from the wilderness to the promised land is covered. That is, the journey from Mount Sinai right over to the promised land is covered by the book of Numbers.

It is very hard to find the theme in the book of Numbers because there are so many parallel themes running through this book. For instance, there is the faithfulness of God and the failure of His people. That is a theme from the beginning to the end of the book—the faithfulness of God and the failure of His people. Then again, you will find that Numbers has another theme: warfare and conflict. From beginning to end there is warfare and conflict. The very first chapter begins with men of war and its last chapters are still talking about the warfare they are in. It is a book of warfare and of conflict. It is a book of probation and trial. Everything is on trial. The greatest man amongst the people of

God is on trial. His brother and his sister are on trial. The priests are on trial. The Levites are on trial. The people of God are on trial. The elders, the rulers, the princes are on trial. Everybody is on trial. They are on probation and every single thing rests upon their absolute obedience. Their obtaining the inheritance, their obtaining the promised land depends upon God proving them after He has tried them in the wilderness.

Then again, another theme in this book from beginning to end is pilgrimage and service. All the way through the book you find pilgrimage. They are not allowed to settle down. It is pilgrimage all the time. We find the book deals with a tremendous amount of service. I think that you will be amazed at the amount that is taken up in this book of the service of God—all the direction in the service of God, how the furniture is carried, who is to carry it, where it is to be carried to, just to find everything proportioned out. The service of God is a very large thing in this book. You see, we find throughout this particular book a large number of themes, which are not just found in one chapter, but are found in the first chapter, the last chapter, and running right through it. So it is very hard to find the theme in such a book.

Then again, we have to recognise that, in this particular book, God has taken another great step forward. I believe that it is in this step forward we find the key to the book of Numbers. God has taken one step forward in Genesis, another step forward in Exodus, a third step in Leviticus, and a fourth step in Numbers. He has taken a very big step forward in Leviticus. He has taken a very big step forward in Numbers. It is found in the first verse of the first chapter. I suppose you have noted that we are always putting a lot of emphasis upon the first verse of the first chapter of each book. Generally speaking, the key to the book is within its first written words.

This book begins like this: "The Lord spake unto Moses in the wilderness of Sinai, in the tent of meeting ..." Some of you may have thought to yourself, "Huh? It opens the same way that the book of Leviticus opens. God was speaking to Moses in the tent of meeting in the book of Leviticus." Ah, you are wrong. The book of Leviticus says, "And the Lord spake unto Moses from out of the tent of meeting." The book of Numbers begins with this: "The Lord spake unto Moses in the tent of meeting."

God has taken a great step forward. For the first time, as far as the written Word goes, we find that God is here dealing with man in His house. Before, He was speaking to man from out of His dwelling place on the whole problem of how they could become part of His dwelling place. Now in Numbers He is dealing with man as in His dwelling place. He is speaking with man as inside the household of God as someone who is responsible toward God for the things of God and the purpose of God in the house of God. He speaks to Moses in the tent of meeting, not from out of it, but in it. He is in it and Moses is in it, and He speaks to Him inside. We will leave the other phrase, "in the wilderness," for a few moments and deal with that a little later.

We shall find that this book tells us that everything depends upon the faithfulness of God and our responsibility, the faithfulness of God and of our taking full responsibility. We shall find as we go through this book that if we fail to take full responsibility that will be the measure in which we fail to reach God's objective.

Authorship and Date of the Writing

Now, let us consider the question of the authorship and the date of this part of the Pentateuch. I think we can say quite simply that it is generally the work of Moses. Humanly speaking, on the human side, Numbers is the work of Moses. There is one problem that you will find in Numbers 12:3. (There are, of course, quite a few problems, but we are not going to deal with technical problems about the authorship of the book.) We understand it to be the work of Moses, but we do read in Numbers 12:3, "Now the man Moses was very meek, above all the men that were upon the face of the earth." Perhaps we do not quite reconcile a man who was so meek with being able to write about himself in that way. I, myself, have absolutely no difficulty whatsoever in believing that a person came, not only to watch over this, but to add the death of Moses in Deuteronomy. I am quite sure that someone may have inserted this and that insertion was undoubtedly as much of the Lord as any other part of the book of Numbers, if indeed Moses did not write it. I, myself, find it a little hard to believe that Moses penned those words about himself.

It would seem that Numbers was written between the 14th and 13th century BC, approximately. It covers a period of about 38–39 years. You will see that this book begins at Sinai and ends at Jordan. You must bear that in mind because, when you come to the book of Deuteronomy, you are going to find that Deuteronomy is going right back over it all, once again, and drawing some very big lessons from it. Deuteronomy has nothing further to do, as far as physical journeys go. This book takes us right up to the other side of the Jordan, over against Jericho. In other words, it brings us to the actual point of them going over the Jordan to possess the promised land. We have to understand that. It covers then a period of about 38 years.

I want you also to note another very interesting point. It is a technical point, but it is an interesting point. These 38 years are split up in a very interesting way. Numbers 1–14, that is the first 14 chapters of Numbers, deal with one year. Then you find that the last 17 chapters of Numbers deal with another single year. The other five chapters deal with something like 37 years. It is a very interesting fact that what is outside the will of God is not recorded. Many people think that the whole of the wilderness wandering in 40 years is recorded in Scripture, whereas, in actual fact, there is a large blank left over very much the larger part of the wilderness wandering. We have only a few places given to us in Numbers 33 which just run over, very briefly, but not fully, all the places where they stopped and encamped.

So, you see that the 36–37 years which take up the major part of this period of time are covered in five chapters. Numbers deals more with the first part of that period and the last part of that period. In other words, it deals very much more fully with them coming right up to the point where they should have gone over to possess the land. Then it deals very much more fully with the last part when, once again, they came up to the point of going over to possess the land.

The Key to the Book of Numbers

What is the key to the book of Numbers? I think you will find the key in two places. One is Numbers 1:1, which simply says,

"The Lord spake unto Moses in the wilderness of Sinai in the tent of meeting." The other is this little phrase in Numbers 12:7, "My servant Moses is not so, he is faithful in all my house." I believe that within these two phrases you have the key to the book of Numbers: "He spake to Moses in the tent of meeting," and "My servant Moses is not so, he is faithful in all My house." Faithful in all My house. This, I say, is the key to the book of Numbers: faithful in all My house. The key is responsibility—responsibility toward the Lord and His house over the things of God. That responsibility is on trial. That is the key to this book. It is that the Lord is looking for a grown-up, adult response and reaction on the part of His people to Himself, to His dwelling place, and to all the things to do with Himself. It is this matter which is of such paramount importance: this whole question of responsibility.

Wherever you turn in Numbers, everything is on trial. It is the youngest and the smallest (at least from the age of responsibility upward) to the eldest in Israel, they are all on trial, everyone. Moses is on trial. Miriam is on trial. Aaron is on trial. The priests are on trial. The Levites are on trial. The princes and the elders are on trial. The whole nation is on trial. The responsible part of the nation, not the new generation, but those that are twenty and older are on trial. This trial is not a trial of those who are too young to be of age. Those who are on probation are those who have reached the age of twenty and upward. In other words, it is a question of responsibility on trial. Not everyone of the children of God are on trial, but responsible people are on probation.

You will note that this book begins and ends, roughly, with a census. In nearly all the commentaries written, people tend to tone down this question of a census. Again and again, commentaries say that we should not take any notice of the Greek title of this book, "Numbers," because it is a very misleading title indeed. It will give you an entirely wrong impression about this part of the Pentateuch. I have read one that said they thought it unfortunate that the Greek scholars rather superficially read this book and decided to call it Numbers. This is nothing of the kind. I think the Greek title, Numbers, is a very good one indeed for the simple reason that everyone who is responsible has been numbered and not one of them is left out. Furthermore, the Holy Spirit has seen fit that the first chapter was taken up with a census of every man over the age of twenty and then again we find in chapter 26 everyone is again numbered. That is, the new generation is again numbered. In other words, the book is bounded by two numberings of the children of Israel. This, I think, has got to be noted if we are to understand this book at all.

A Symbol of Responsibility

We also find another interesting point about the book of Numbers. The Levites occupied probably a larger place in the book of Numbers than maybe in the book of Leviticus. If you have read the book of Numbers, even superficially, you must have been impressed by the way the Levites are continually mentioned. All the time the Levites are coming in. If it is not their cities, it is their offering. If it is not their offering, it is their separation. If it is not their separation, it is their function. If it is not their function, it is their nature. But everywhere through this book, again and again you come back to the Levites. You are all the time coming back to the Levites and you should know that, in Scripture, the Levites signify responsibility. They are always a symbol of responsibility toward the Lord and His people.

Three Strands in Responsibility

So you see that the key to this book is one that is, in many ways, a very, very wonderful one. We find three things in the book of Numbers. The first is responsibility, the second is probation and the third is rebellion. These three things always go together. You might think I am very emphatic to say these three things always go together, but they always go together: responsibility, probation, and rebellion. Whenever the Lord has given responsibility in a people, He will always have rebellion. Always. It is the reaction of man's old nature to responsibility. In other words, it is irresponsibility over against responsibility. It nearly always comes from those who ought to be responsible, but are rebelling against being responsible. So, you find the Lord numbering all from twenty years upward. Then you find He puts them all on trial. Then the book of Numbers is the awful story, the tragic story of the vast number failing in their responsibility, and indeed, failing at every opportunity against the Lord in this matter of whether they should take responsibility.

Right the way through, you find these three strands woven together. The Lord putting grown up children of His into a place of responsibility and then testing them, trying them on every single point and we find that the answer is always a purging, a purifying, or rebellion.

I think it is very, very interesting that the book of Numbers should have so much to do with rebellion. You find that chapters 9–25 are really one continuous story of rebellion from beginning to end. It is just an awful story of rebellion. Many of us smiled when we first came to the Lord and read these scriptures. I know I did. I used to find it very, very amusing. I had never heard anything like it. I would read one page and I would find they had murmured. I would look at the next paragraph and find they had murmured again. I would turn another page and find they had murmured again. I found the Lord dealt with them and they murmured against His dealing. When He settled an issue, they murmured against Him. They cannot be quiet; they must murmur. All the time they murmur. I used to think when I was much younger in the Lord, that this is really amusing. Until I found through bitter experience that this is absolutely true.

Human beings are the most amazing murmurers, and I do believe the Lord's people are the very worst of all murmurers. It seems to me that when the Lord deals with us in any way whatsoever you have the greatest amount of murmuring, back chat, gainsaying, contradiction, haggling and all this sort of thing that goes on with all kinds of the Lord's people. Even when the Lord settles the issue, it slowly comes back again. Here then we find the key to this book, but shining through it all the faithfulness of God.

One of the most wonderful parts of this book to me is the part dealing with Balaam. There in the plain, the people were murmuring. In the plain they are rebelling. They are tired with Moses. They are tired with the way that they are going. They are tired with their food, which is God's provision. They are tired.

In every way they are tired. They are tired of the ministry, tired of the leadership, tired of the vestry, tired of the history. They are just weary of it all. They are groaning and moaning, not only about Moses, and about Aaron, and the priests, but also about the Lord Himself. Yet, the Lord tells Balaam, "I haven't even seen perverseness in the tents of Jacob" (see Numbers 23:21). He speaks of the Lord's property as being so beautiful, so upright, all righteous. I think this is just an indication of the faithfulness of God over His own people even when they are amazingly filled with rebellion and failure.

Now, let us look a little bit more closely at this. You see, there we can find an outline. The first eight chapters deal basically with this question of responsibility. Then we will find that chapters 9–25 deal with responsibility on trial. That is the whole period to do with the outcome of all the rebellion. The last chapters, 26–36, are the re-numbering, the new census of a new generation and the last commandment the Lord gives before they go over the Jordan into the promised land.

#1 Responsibility: In Tremendous Conflict

Now, we will look at these first few chapters of Numbers together. In chapters one, two, three, and four, we find three basic things about responsibility. The first is this: a tremendous conflict will always wage on this earth, until the Lord returns, over God's dwelling place. It is the one thing that Satan, from the beginning, has set himself against. He is more set against the dwelling place of God than even our personal salvation. He is against our personal salvation because he knows our personal salvation will lead to our becoming incorporated into God's house. This caused pride to be found in Satan at the very beginning. It is something that he has been set against ever since. A tremendous conflict then rages over the dwelling place of God. It is very interesting that whenever you touch anything to do with the church that affects us in a practical way, there are always explosions and reactions which are not just human and physical. It is because the enemy is set against God finding His rest and satisfaction in a people. He is against that house built from the living stones. That is at the heart of this conflict. It does not matter where we are, we shall find at Zion, or Jerusalem, or the temple, or the tabernacle, or the church of the living God, wherever we go we shall find that this is the heart of the conflict. This is the focal point of the conflict. The book of Revelation reveals only too clearly to us that the testimony of Jesus is the focal point of all the vilest and most ferocious attacks and assaults at the end.

You see, responsibility is a matter to do with warfare. I am always amazed when people are frightened in scraps and fights. Why do Christians always want to have it all peaceful and sweet? As soon as there is the slightest scrap, they vanish as if they cannot stick it, as if it is not right. Warfare anywhere, outside the house or inside the house, believe me, is part of the conflict. Furthermore, you and I have been numbered to be part of that conflict. If we try to get out of it, we are proving to be irresponsible. Our place, our part, is to be in this battle. The armour is given for us all, not for a few. It is given for everyone who has come to spiritual age. We all ought to be in the battle. If we are somehow bypassing the battle, if we are trying to evade or avoid the battle, then we are just proving that we are going to fall and lose our inheritance. Hebrews is a book that speaks of the possibility—not of losing our salvation—but of losing our inheritance, of losing all that the Lord has saved us into, but we will not lose our salvation.

Here you have it again. This question of the dwelling place of God involves us in a mortal conflict. It is a conflict which is unto blood, a conflict which is real, a conflict which never ceases down here. You and I have been numbered by the Lord for this conflict. We are numbered for it. But if you want to stay in the babyhood stage all your life, you will not be in the conflict. If you wish to remain in the nursery, you will not be in the conflict. God's thought is that you could be a man of war. You should be one of the men of war that is numbered here in the book of Numbers.

Here is where we begin to deal with the basic nature of responsibility. It is to do with warfare. God wants men and women who can get out into the battle on this question of His house, people who can go out, through whom God can achieve something on this question of His house.

#2 Responsibility: A Life Position

Then again, you will find there is something else in chapter two. Everything is a question of right position, of encampment. The second thing we learn about responsibility is simply that it is a life position and attitude. You know these people who one minute are talking about the house, talking about fellowship, talking about relationship but the next minute they are gone. They are not here. You look for them. You need them. They are not here. They are gone. They have decided that they ought to be somewhere else, that they should be off here, or off there, or over there. This Christian responsibility involves a basic life position and attitude.

Here I would like to show you something, which some of the older ones will be very well acquainted with, but of which others of you may not be so well acquainted. In Numbers 2, everything is bound up with the position the people take regarding God and His dwelling place. Everything is around the dwelling place. Nothing is left for self-opinion. Nothing is left to corporate self-opinion. Nothing is left to conglomeration of view. Nothing is left to self-will. Nothing! Everything is apportioned by God. Each tribe is important—Issachar, Judah, Zebulon, Asher, Dan, Naphtali, Benjamin, Ephraim, Manasseh, Simeon, Reuben, and Gad. All of them have been given their place and, within each tribe, the princes of the tribe are to apportion each man the place for his tent. All should be in order. Everything should be, as it were, in military order. Then you find the Kohathites, the Gershonites, and the Merarites are being camped around the ark, around the tabernacle, as well as Moses, Aaron and his sons, that is, the priesthood of the Israelites.

This then, teaches us that responsibility involves us in a life position regarding God's dwelling place. That is, whether we are washing, or looking after the children, or shopping, or at business, or earning our wage so that others can live upon it, or whether we are wholly involved in the things of God—whatever it is—our life position is to be related to the house of God at the centre. It is not our home and the house of God around it, not our home and the Lord's blessing, not our job and the Lord's helping us. It is our job, our home, our life, our career, our business, everything found in its proper relationship to the dwelling place of God.

The house of God is at the heart of the people. It is a life position. You cannot change it. You must keep to your position. It is something to be kept. It is something to be adhered to. There are penalties attached to not adhering. Your place was found to be there. If anyone thought that they ought to be a Levite and wandered into the place where the Levites had stood–they may die! Keep them away. There is to be no disorder, no confusion. Everyone must keep to the place appointed to him of God.

So you see, responsibility not only involves us in warfare—that unseen, terrible, satanic warfare, but it also involves us in a life position. No one can be responsible who thinks that everything should centre around him or her, or around their business, around their lives, around their home. Your home, your business, your career, everything of yours has to find its place in relation to God and His dwelling place at the centre. That is, the house of God has to be the heart and the hub of your life. That, you will understand, is not a place of brick and mortar, but the house made up of living stones. You need to fully understand that.

#3 Responsibility: Its Essential Nature

In chapters three and four, you find the essential nature of responsibility. It is not only a question of conflict, not only a life position, but an attitude ... by the way, everyone is included in that, even the babies, even the irresponsible. The one who cannot take responsibility is included in the encampment. Everyone who is there has to find their place. That is how they will come to responsibility. So even if some of you fear that you are not yet responsible, you still have to put the Lord and His dwelling place at the heart so that you might become responsible.

You find in chapters three and four that you have the basic nature of responsibility. You have the Levites. You have the Levites numbered. Now, this is a new numbering. The Levites were never numbered with the men of war. They have their own peculiar function. This function is summed up in three things. You will find one in Numbers 4:23 and in 8:24. In the margin, it reads like this: "war the warfare in the work." This was the job of the Levites: warring the warfare in the work. Their job was inside the house, the service of God. You will find that that was usually those from 30 to 50 years of age.

Then, after age 50, they passed into another category, which we find mentioned in Numbers 8:25,26: "keeping the charge." Here you have the most physical service. In their younger, strong days, they entered upon it at the age of 30. They had a five-year apprenticeship with a Levite. From 25–30 he was apprenticed. At 30 he entered upon his service, his work and then at 50 he passed over into "keeping the charge" over the work of God.

However, I found something which perhaps goes to the heart of Levitical service more than anything else. It is a little phrase found in Numbers 4:47: "bearing the burden." They shall be bearing the burden. It is not bearing the burdens that are personal, so do not comfort yourself if you have big, personal burdens that you feel you are carrying — it doesn't say that. No, these burdens are the burdens of the house of God. Levites have grown up out of petty self-consciousness and petty self-centredness. They reveal to us the essential nature of responsibility, which is Christ-centred.

They reveal to us simply that the essential nature of responsibility is to bear burdens bigger than our own.

Do you know there are many Christians who have completely succumbed under their own burden? They have never learned the secret that to bear the burdens of the Lord is to find release from your own. Whether they be personal problems to do with your own personality, to do with your own history, to do with your own circumstances, to do with your own relationships, whatever it is—it is a question of bearing the burdens of the Lord. If you encompass that, you will find that your own burdens, in their end, will find their solution, if only that you have found the Lord to be your strength.

Here we find the Levites, and the Levites are carefully apportioned to their work. If you are a Kohathite you have a certain job. If you are Gershonite you have a certain job. If you are a Merarite you have a certain job. If I am a Merarite I cannot do the Kohathite's job. If I do, I may die. This is a question of order.

Editors Note: We apologise to the reader for the abrupt conclusion, but the audio of this message was cut short. We are thankful to have the study guide on hand, which is an outline of Numbers that Lance edited. We trust that this will provide good 'nuggets' which will fill in the gaps and shed further light on this book of Numbers. Please see the study guide following. You will note that some sections have been covered in the chapter. However, the material in the guide elaborates on many of the points.

12.
Numbers
Study Guide

Introduction

The name "Numbers" is taken from the Greek, and is derived from the fact that, on two occasions, a census was taken (Numbers 1–4 and 26) the first at Sinai, and the second on the banks of the Jordan. The Hebrew title comes from the opening sentence of the book, "In the wilderness," and this title is the more appropriate title of the two, as we shall see.

Numbers describes events before and after the wanderings in the wilderness (of which we have little knowledge), taking us from Mt. Sinai, where the book of Exodus ends, to the borders of Canaan, at the River Jordan, near Jericho, where Joshua begins. It takes us right up to the point prior to the crossing into the promised land.

In Numbers, we find that God has taken another step in the realising of His purpose—He speaks not "out of the tent of meeting" to Moses, but He speaks to Moses "in the tent of meeting." For the first time, we are viewed as being within the house of God, in a responsible way, and we are also shown that everything depends upon His faithfulness and our responsibility.

Authorship and Date

The book of Numbers is generally the work of Moses. "The Lord spoke unto Moses ..." (Numbers 1:1) "... which the Lord commanded by the hand of Moses ..." (Numbers 36:13). It was written somewhere between BC 1440–1300 and covers a period of about 38 years, as can be seen from the following dates:

- Numbers 1:1: "1st day of 12th month in the 2nd year" (compare Exodus 40:17)
- Numbers 10:11: "20th day of the 2nd month in the 2nd year" the cloud lifted
- Numbers 33:38: "1st day of the 5th month in the 40th year" Aaron dies
- Deuteronomy 1:3: "1st day of the 11th month in the 40th year" Moses' farewell

Notice that no dates are given between the 2nd and 40th years. This book can be chronologically divided into the following:

Numbers 1–14: 1 year

Numbers 15–20: 36–37 years

Numbers 20–36: 1 year

It is interesting to note that the wilderness wanderings, for the most part, are not on record.

The Key to the Book

In Numbers, it is hard to find the key, for we find so much running though it: God's faithfulness and our failure, warfare and conflict, rebellion and division, pilgrimage and service, trial and probation. In Numbers 1:1 and 12:7, however, we find what it is that God is drawing to our attention "... in the wilderness ... in the tent of meeting ... and he is faithful in all Mine House."

It appears that responsibility is the key—responsibility toward the Lord, responsibility over the things of God. This responsibility, furthermore, is on probation, and wherever we turn in Numbers, we discover that all are on trial as to this question—Moses, Aaron, Miriam, the priests, the Levites, the princes, elders, and the people.

We ought to note that the book begins and ends with a numbering of the people from 20 years old, and upward. This reveals the desire and intention of God that all should grow up, and take full responsibility for, and in, God's house. Taking inward and practical responsibility for the things of God and the people of God, for His dwelling place is, in fact, the heart of true service. We ought to note also that the Levites occupy a very prominent place in this book. In the Bible, they always represent responsibility in the house of God. Their service toward God, in an especial way, began with the incident in Exodus 32:25–29, compare Numbers 3:11–13

We see then, in Numbers, three things—responsibility, probation, and rebellion, but shining through all, the faithfulness of God (see Psalm 78 for a commentary on Numbers).

The Outline of the Book

I. Responsibility

Dealt with Basically (Numbers 1–8

  A. The conflict over the house of God (Numbers 1:1–54)

      1. All are responsible in this warfare (Numbers 1:2, 3)

      2. The Levites—especial case (Numbers 1:47–54)

  B. The position of the house of God (Numbers 2:1–34)

      1. The house of God is central.

      All homes to be in right relation to the dwelling place of God. (Numbers 2:2)

      2. This is to be the fundamental position and attitude for our life.

      3. Note that nothing is left to chance, or self-will, or self-opinion.

      Everything has its place and order. Everyone has his function. Every home and business has to be rightly related to the Lord.

  C. The Nature of Responsibility (Numbers 3:1–8:26)

      1. The especial numbering of the Levites (Numbers 3:14) (compare chapter 1:47–50)

      2. They represent the heart of the matter; warring the warfare in the work (Numbers 4:23; 8:24). The Hebrew uses a word connected with war, or armies, often translated as "hosts"; keeping the charge (Numbers 8:26); bearing the burdens (Numbers 4:47)

  D. Responsibility and sin (Numbers 5:1–31)

The leper; trespass against the Lord; jealousy over wife.

E. The motive for tasking responsibility (Numbers 6:1–7:88). It must be from a heart of love, freely offered.

    1. The nazarite vow (Numbers 6:1–21). This is freely entered into, but once made, it must be wholly observed.

    2. The prince's offering (Numbers 7:10–88).
    This was a free will offering made to the
    Lord. Note that it was connected with the altar.
    All true giving must start with the cross. It is
    not for self-exhibition, or self-advance.

F. Responsibility for the lampstand and the Levites' separation (Numbers 7:89–8:26).

Holding the testimony of Jesus costs everything. It means an utter separation to the Lord.

II. Responsibility on Trial

(Numbers 9–25)

A. Divine provision for the Journey (Numbers 9–10)

    1. The passover kept (Numbers 9:1–14)
    The finished work of Christ basic to all.

    2. The pillar of cloud (Numbers 9:15–23).
    The guidance and ministry of the Holy Spirit essential.

    3. The silver trumpets (Numbers 10:1–10)
    The togetherness of God's people always vital.

B. Responsibility and Rebellion

    1. The orderly departure from Mt. Sinai
    (Numbers 10:11–36)

    2. The burning fire (Numbers 11:1–3)

3. The murmuring (70 elders, quails, plague) (Numbers 11:4–35)

4. The rebellion of Miriam and Aaron (Numbers 12:1–16)

5. The spies sent out and the people's reaction (Numbers 13:1–14:45) the evil report of ten, the other spirit of Joshua and Caleb; Moses tested; the pronouncement that the ten will die in the wilderness; the people's presumption.

6. Reiteration (Numbers 15:1–41) provision for the sin; the need for utterness; the need for the fringes of blue (stops fraying and disintegration—blue, to remind them of their heavenly vocation).

7. The rebellion of Korah, Dathan, and Abram (Numbers 16:1–17:2) Note that they were Levites and Reubenites who formed this faction. It was a rebellion over government and ministry. The earth swallowed, the fire destroyed. This resulted in a rebellion of the people. The rod that budded (vindication of divinely vested authority).

8. The provision for the priests and Levites and the provision made for contact with death (Numbers 18:1–19:22). The latter provision for the contamination and defilement which come from touch with dead things—this world.

9. Miriam dies, the people rebel, Moses falls (Numbers 20:1–13)

10. Three Canaanite tribes destroyed
(Numbers 21:1–35). The people rebel again
(the fiery serpents—the brazen serpent)

11. The subtle attempt to deceive Israel
(Numbers 22:1–25:18). Balaam, people
fall, another plague

III. Responsibility Inheriting

(Numbers 26–36)

A. The new generation numbered (Numbers 26:1–65)

B. The laws of inheritance (Numbers 27:1–11)

C. The appointment of Joshua (Numbers 27:12–23)

D. The laws concerning offerings and vows
Restated to the New Generation (Numbers 28:1–30:16)

E. The Midianites slaughtered (Numbers 31:1–54)

F. Reuben, Gad and half the tribe of Manasseh settle down on the wrong side of the Jordan (Numbers 32:1–42)

G. The journey in retrospect (Numbers 33:1–56)

H. The division of Canaan, Levitical cities, cities of refuge (Numbers 34:1–36:13)

The Message of the Book

God's purpose and longing can never be realised without our growing up and taking full responsibility in His House. Responsibility, however, requires intensive probation and testing. Hence the record of the trial and failure of the people at Kadesh (holy) Barnea, when they refused to enter the land of their inheritance which resulted in the consequent judgment on that generation, except for Caleb and Joshua. It also explains the record of murmuring, unbelief, wandering, failure and disobedience, so frequently evidenced in the journey from Kadesh to the plains of Moab. One kind of man was being tested and rejected. Another kind of man was attested, trained and accepted. It was this kind of man who, by the grace of God, was to inherit the land.

We are also taught here that nothing is left to us, to our own wills or to our own opinions or ideas. We see that the Lord is Lord of His house, and has absolute and sovereign right over His own. It is this fact, more than any other, that brings light to the rebellion in us. Nevertheless, given a heart that is for Him, and a settled life position concerning His dwelling place, He in faithfulness will bring us through all the trials of our faith to a full inheritance.

Recommended Books

Notes on Numbers
    C.H. Mackintosh
Exodus and the Wandering in the Wilderness
    A. Edersheim

Questions

1. What was it that God wanted Moses and Aaron to find out when He commanded them to number the people in chapter 1?

Why do you think this needed to be done?

2. Why is it that Numbers 15–20, covering a period of about 37 years, is given so little attention in this book?

3. Read and note what these passages tell you about the Lord Jesus Christ?
a) Numbers 20:2–11

b) Numbers 21:4–9

4. Read chapters 3 and 4. What can you find out about responsibility for the things of the Lord from these chapters? Can you see any lessons for us as the church of Jesus Christ in chapters 3 and 4?

5. Write a history of murmuring and rebellion as it is found in Numbers 11–12, giving reasons for the murmurings and rebellions. Can you learn any lessons for the Christian life and for church life from these chapters?

6. What can you find out about responsible leadership from the following passages:
a) Numbers 9:1–8

b) Numbers 11:10–17

c) Numbers 14:1–25

d) Numbers 15:32–41

e) Numbers 16:20–24, 41–44

f) Numbers 27:1–5, 12–23

7. What do you learn about guidance from 9:15–23, 10:11–13, 34 and 12:5? Why do you think God sent the cloud to cover the tabernacle?

8. Read Numbers 13, 14 and 33:50–56. Compare also Hebrews chapters 3 and 4. Write down some reasons why it is so important that all of us enter into the promises in Christ that God has given to His people.

9. What do you find to be the most disturbing lesson in the book of Numbers?

What do you find to be the most comforting lesson in the book of Numbers?

10. What was it in the hearts of Joshua and Caleb that caused God to choose them, to lead the new generation into the promised land (chapter 13, 14)?

11. In a few sentences, state how the faithfulness of God is revealed in the book of Numbers.

13.
Deuteronomy: Summing up the Pentateuch

There is a tremendous amount about this book of Deuteronomy which is different from the other four books or parts of the Pentateuch. Its aim is somewhat different and its context is different. It is often likened to John's Gospel. The relationship of Deuteronomy to the other four books—Genesis, Exodus, Leviticus, and Numbers, is often likened to the relationship of John's Gospel to Matthew, Mark, and Luke. Matthew, Mark, and Luke are history; John is an interpretation. Genesis, Exodus Leviticus, and Numbers are history; Deuteronomy is an interpretation. John's gospel is a spiritual interpretation and an underlining of the life and significance of the Lord Jesus. Deuteronomy is a spiritual interpretation and an underlining of God's dealing and ways with His people from their beginning.

Deuteronomy in many ways is quite different to the others. We expect it to be different. Even in a superficial reading of the four gospels, they reveal to us a real and essential difference between the whole style and method of the fourth gospel compared to the other three. So, the style and method of Deuteronomy are quite different to the other four books of the Pentateuch. Furthermore, Deuteronomy is prophetical. It is prophetical literature. What do we mean? We mean simply that Deuteronomy is not a book of laws like Leviticus or parts of Exodus. It is not a book of simple clear teaching like, shall we say again, Leviticus or Exodus. It is not even history like Genesis or Numbers. Deuteronomy is prophetical. We mean that it is the interpretation of history and it is the interpretation of the laws and regulations. Teaching is one thing; prophecy is another.

Deuteronomy is Prophetical

In the New Testament, we have different gifts. We have the teacher and we have the prophet. The ministry and function of the teacher is quite distinct from that of the prophet. Deuteronomy is the interpretation of the past, the present, and the future. It is, therefore, prophetical. There are some people who think very wrongly and misguidedly that prophecy is all to do with the future. I suggest to such people that they should do a very real study in the Bible of prophecy because you will often find that prophecy has a lot to do with the past, and an even good deal more to do with the present. If you think of Isaiah and others, you find that they are often interpreting past events, as well as future happenings, and much to do with the present.

So here we find that Deuteronomy is prophetical. By that we mean that it is taking up past history and present experience, as well as the future, and interpreting it to the people. We have already seen Moses as the lawgiver. We have seen Moses as ruler.

Now we see Moses as a prophet. Indeed, the one name perhaps above every other name given to Moses is that of prophet. Deuteronomy, therefore, reveals to us the heart of Moses. If you want any book in the Bible which is a spontaneous, and in some ways, as far as Moses is concerned, one book which reveals a man's heart (although he didn't mean to reveal himself; it was not deliberate), it is this book of Deuteronomy.

I suppose we would all agree that you will hardly find anything in the Bible to excel the beauty and loveliness of Deuteronomy. Some of the most beautiful phrases in the whole Word of God are found within this book. Indeed, it has often been hailed as one of the greatest pieces of literature of all human history. Deuteronomy certainly has something different from Genesis, Exodus, Leviticus, and Numbers in the beauty of its style, and not only the beauty of its style, but also the beauty of its language.

One is very much reminded (and this, by the way, is just an aside) of Moses' authorship of Deuteronomy when reading Psalm 90 and 91 because they can be read as commentaries on one another. They betray the same beauty and majesty of phrase. Moses seemed to have a sweep about him; about his language and about the way he defined and set forth things. I think sometimes we do Moses a great injustice by considering him to be a very hard man, a sort of legal, technical type of man; Deuteronomy reveals a very different kind of Moses. It reveals a man who at one moment may be full of the most majestic and fiery indignation, but at the next moment is full of very real gentleness and love. So, at any rate we find that there is something quite different about this book of Deuteronomy.

Another point that I hope you have noticed while reading it is the direct simplicity of its language. I do not know how many of you have read Deuteronomy, but I think you will all be quite surprised by the direct way in which it is written. You will always get this kind of thing: "We did so-and-so and so-and-so." He says, "You remember that we came to such and such a point." This is the language of a man who is speaking amongst friends about events that were known to them all. That is why Deuteronomy is so very thrilling to read as a document, forgetting the chapters, forgetting the verses, just reading it through from beginning to end. If you have the time, it will not take you all that long. You will be very struck by the style and the simple, direct language that is used.

Then we should take note of one or two technical facts. This book is the most quoted in the New Testament than all the other volumes of the Old Testament. There is no other book in the whole Old Testament more quoted in the New Testament than the book of Deuteronomy. It is also a very strange thing that there has been no book in the Bible more attacked than the book of Deuteronomy. Now, those of you who know anything about Biblical criticism will know that Deuteronomy is the one that has suffered more at the hand of higher critics than anything else in the Bible. They have split it up, torn it apart, bashed its so-called authorship and done everything they can to discredit Deuteronomy.

Deuteronomy is quoted or alluded to approximately 96 times in the New Testament. In the Old Testament, it is quoted or eluded to 356 times. Another interesting fact is that it is intimately bound up, obviously, with the four preceding books. We find that it quotes Genesis 30 times, Exodus 94 times, Leviticus 61 times, and Numbers 74 times. So this book of Deuteronomy sums up the Pentateuch. It goes back over the other four books and sums them up, interprets them, underlines the principle, and emphasises what the Lord is really after. That is why the rest of the Bible takes so much from Deuteronomy.

It is an interesting point that when the Devil came to the Lord Jesus and tempted Him, He answered him three times out of Deuteronomy. He never went to any other book for His answers. He said three times, "It is written" and each time He referred the Devil back to the book of Deuteronomy. The old Puritans used to say that like David and Goliath the Lord Jesus took five pebbles: Genesis, Exodus, Leviticus, Numbers, and Deuteronomy. He only used one: Deuteronomy, and the one killed Goliath. So that is just something for you to think about. The Lord Jesus only used Deuteronomy. He triumphed by His knowledge of this one part of the Pentateuch and it says, "The Devil left Him."

Authorship and Date

Now, what about its authorship and its date? The first thing is that it is manifestly the work of Moses. In Deuteronomy 31:24–26a, we find this: "And it came to pass, when Moses had made an end of writing the words of this law in a book, until they were finished, that Moses commanded the Levites, that bare the ark of the covenant of Jehovah, saying, Take this book of the law …"

"This book of the law" is the book of the law that we believe King Josiah found when he removed the rubbish from the temple. Do you remember? He rediscovered the book of the law by the altar.

Thus the book itself proclaims to be the work, humanly speaking, of Moses. Possibly, as we mentioned about Numbers, there are a few additions. It is very interesting to note in the Revised Version, the parenthesis there are in this book. Now and again you find in brackets just a few comments about what this could be or that could be, which might well be the work of another scribe, nevertheless, inspired. Then, of course, I think most would agree that the last few chapters of Deuteronomy were probably written by someone else, possibly Joshua or someone else. Again, I know that some of the old Puritans used to believe that Moses was so inspired that he wrote the account of his own death. Whilst I do not for a moment question the possibility of a man being given such a vision since he had been given a vision of so much else, I think it is probably more likely that Joshua compiled the last few chapters of this book of Deuteronomy.

When was it written? Here is something I think is of tremendous interest. It was written a month before the death of Moses. So this book was written in the 120th year of Moses' life and it was written at the very end of his life. We are told expressly that Moses' vigour, Moses' soundness had not in any way diminished. He was at the end of his life as full of health and soundness in strength and ability as he was when he was a young man. So it is not surprising we have here then documents written within a month of the death of Moses and probably within two months of the children of Israel crossing over into the land. In a sense, if you can read Deuteronomy with that background, it makes it much more thrilling. Here is something coming out of a man who has been used of God, who has a long, worn out history with God going back 120 years. Eighty years of that 120 years are the most vivid and deep history. Now, just before he is about to die and just at the very threshold of people journeying into the land to possess it, he gathers them together and speaks to them these last words.

It was written in the uplands of Moab. In those days, it would have been very fertile and green, and overlooked the plain of Jordan, and particularly Jericho, so that the people sat while Moses taught them, instructed them, and interpreted their history and their laws to them in sight of the promised land. That was roughly, something around 1400 BC.

The Key to the Book

What is the key to the book of Deuteronomy? Most of you know that its Greek title just means: "second law giving," or, even better, to give its real meaning, it is: "the repetition of the law." Deuteronomy is a repetition of the law. It is the giving again of the law. Its Hebrew title is once again taken from the very first few words in chapter one: "These are the words." This is the Hebrew title of Deuteronomy: "these are the words," or "the repetition of the law, the second law giving."

Although we are not going to emphasise so much this side, we, as children of God, ought to take note of the words of God. When the Lord speaks to us it is tremendously important. We should always be careful of any kind of despising or belittling of the Word of God in any shape or form. You remember that so much happened to the children of Israel because they despised the Word of the Lord given by Moses. We must remember that. If you have read through the book of Deuteronomy, you will have noticed, I am quite sure, the emphasis that there is upon the Word of the Lord. Moses is continually saying to them, "Remember, the Lord spake to you." He is continually saying this: "The Lord spake to you. You saw Him speak out of the cloud. Thick darkness, the cloud, the darkness was there and He spake to you out of it". So we have to take note of the Word of God.

The key, however, to Deuteronomy is not the Word of God, or ministry, however great and wonderful that is. Why do you think the Greek title is "The Repetition of the Law," "The Second Law Given"? Why do you think the Hebrew title is "These are the words" with the evident thought of going back over something, talking about something? Surely, the key to this book is that there is an essential element and quality that the Lord is looking for, and which alone can answer Him, which, if it is not there, renders everything else obsolete—spurious, which if it is there, with perhaps much weakness, much frailty, means that the Lord can move forward and accomplish His purpose.

I believe emphatically—truly emphatically—that Deuteronomy has its place in the Word of God, with all its repetition of that which had already been given, just because the Lord wants us to go right to the root of the whole matter. The Lord is so concerned that He has given us a whole book which takes up much which has already been spoken. It seems a waste of time. The Lord takes up history, which we have already got. He takes up law, which we have already got. He takes up a covenant which has already been made and He restates the whole thing. But why? Because the Lord is looking for an essential element which alone can satisfy Him. In other words, the Lord can have a people, He can have them in the land, He can have the services, He can have the regulations, He can have a national life, a national character, a national vocation as such, and yet, it all would just be empty as far as He is concerned. It is built according to pattern. It is built on the law that He has given. It is observing the statutes that He has given, and yet, the essential element, which alone can satisfy His heart, is missing. Because that one element is missing, the Lord is dissatisfied. He is not satisfied. He is not answered. It does not correspond to Him. Do you understand what I mean? It does not meet Him. It does not answer to His nature. I think, you see, that it is touching the root of this book, and the root of this book is love. That is the essential element that the Lord is looking for.

Many people like to think that the Old Testament is altogether void of love. They like to think that it is all a question of law and regulation, shadows and symbols. But we make a great mistake. The Lord's nature has not changed from that dispensation to this dispensation. God is love. Patterns, regulations, a kept law, and observed ordinances cannot possibly ever satisfy the heart of God. They may satisfy religious people, but they cannot satisfy the heart of a living God.

God's Essential Nature

God's essential nature is love. Therefore, He has to find something that corresponds to Him, that answers to Him, that can meet Him. Therefore, that means He has to find love. Love can only meet love. Love cannot be satisfied by duty in another. Love cannot be satisfied by sheer apish obedience in others. Love cannot be satisfied by just an observance of ordinances in others. Love requires love. Love must have love. Love, you see, will never rest till it gets love. That love can only be answered by love. Thus, you see, this book is written with that in mind. The key to this whole book is love.

Now, I am going to surprise you, I think. Do you know that love between God and men and men and God is hardly mentioned in the Bible until Deuteronomy? In only one place is love mentioned: Exodus 20:6: "... them that love me and keep my commandments." That is all. It is the only mention. You search it. I am not saying that love is not illustrated in those books. I am not saying that love is not implied in those books. It is implied from the beginning. What I am saying is that love is not explicitly revealed in so many words.

The Love of God

Deuteronomy, if you take a concordance and look at it, is full of love. Everywhere it is love. The main aspects of love are God's love for us and our love for God, and then our love for one another. Of course, if you want to look up the word "love," you will find that Isaac loved Rebecca, and Jacob loved Joseph, and other quotations about love. However, it is interesting that you will not find once in Genesis, Exodus, Leviticus, and Numbers the mention of the love of God. Not once! God's love for us, for humanity, is not even mentioned in those four books. He waits till the book of Deuteronomy before He starts to speak about His love for us. Only once does He speak of our love for Him when He gave the Ten Commandments, and then in an aside. You will see that it just says this in Exodus 20:6: "... showing lovingkindness unto thousands of them that love Me and keep My commandments." It is just that part of the Ten Commandments, "showing lovingkindness unto thousands of them that love Me and keep My commandments." That is the only mention of love for the Lord.

So, you see, I think we have discovered the key to the book of Deuteronomy. Why does the Lord go over the law again? Why does He again define the covenant? Why does He go through a review of their history? Because He wants to define an essential quality without which He can never be satisfied.

This is why John's Gospel is linked with Deuteronomy in so many ways. Everywhere in the book of Deuteronomy we find the basic necessity for love. Everywhere. For instance, for the first time we find that behind all God's dealings with us is His love. This Moses spake very clearly. He said, "He loves you." He loves you, not because of anything, He just loves you. It is not because you were better, not because you were the most, not even because you were a minority. He just loved you and because He loved you, He chose you.

Then he begins to depict their history. Do you know about Balaam? Do you know that the Ammonites hired Balaam to come to you? Do you know why the Lord confounded Balaam? Because He loves you (see Deuteronomy 23:4–5). Well, we never knew that before. Now we are discovering what lies behind history. God loves His people. All through this book of Deuteronomy we are beginning to find that behind their history is God's great love. In the same way, we can take great encouragement in the things we do not understand, the many things we do not even know, we shall one day discover that behind them all is the love of God.

So you see it is simply that this book shows us, reveals to us that behind all God's dealings—from the beginning right the way through that thin line of the good seed, down to Abraham, Isaac, and Jacob, to Moses, to a people, and right the way through, now forty years in the wilderness—the love of God has been behind everything. It has been fashioning, moulding, leading, guiding, instructing, preserving within the love of God.

We find also that nothing can satisfy God but perfect love, and something more which I think will interest us all. Moses tells us repeatedly that love is the answer for our security and preservation. He is, in virtual fact, saying to the people of God, if you love the Lord, you will be kept in the ways and the will of God. If you just slavishly obey the Lord, you may fail. You may fall. But if you love the Lord, you will find that He will keep you in His will and His way. His way is love. That is why the Lord is always after love, and why He is so afraid of our first love declining because He knows that when love goes, there is the possibility of every kind of evil. Love is not just the only thing that can satisfy God, but it is also the means by which God can keep us in His ways and in His will.

To Love the Lord

Then I want you also to notice how the book of Deuteronomy developed some other words from this word love. You will find quite a little series of words that recur more than once: to obey, to cleave, to serve, and to fear the Lord. They all come out of this word to love the Lord. They are always found somehow in connection with the word of loving the Lord. Obeying the Lord, cleaving to the Lord, serving the Lord and fearing the Lord are bound up in love. Does this not somehow put the toll, if I may use the word, into this whole question of obedience and service? Do you see, what the Lord is simply saying is that the centre of it all, the heart of it all is love. Understand that, and out of that will come obedience which is lifetime obedience and out of that will come the fear of the Lord.

Do you know what fear of the Lord is? It is not a terrible thing. Fear of the Lord is a reverence for the Lord, a gentle fear of doing anything that could somehow upset or grieve the Lord. It is a tender conscience, a sensitive nature to anything important to Him. This is fearing the Lord and it comes out of love. If you love a person, you will fear them in a right way. Somehow or other, you cannot know why, you know they cannot do such and such. But you love them very much and they love you very much and you want to abide together. You see, it is not a slavish fear; it is a gentle understanding of another person's sensitivity in the matter. This is what it means to fear the Lord. There is something that we can do but we don't because we know that the loving Holy Spirit wouldn't have us do it that way. We know it would upset the Lord, if we are very, very sensitive to the Lord.

All these things come out of this one question of love. If you love a person you cleave to them. You cannot let them go (in a right way). You will cleave to them. It is like Ruth said to her mother-in-law: "Where you go, I go. Where you live, I live. Where you die, I die. Where you are buried, I am buried." She was cleaving to her mother-in-law. That is the same with us. If we love the Lord we will cleave to Him. Where He goes, we will go. None of this question of: "I must follow the Lamb withersoever He goeth. I must do it! Oh dear, it is so awful, but I must." We love the Lord, so we shall cleave to the Lord. Withersoever the Lord goes, we go. We shall say to Him just the same. "Where You go, I go. Where You live, I live. Where You die, I die. Where You are buried, I am buried." We cleave to the Lord.

A History of Experience and Observation

I want you to notice a very wonderful thing. Moses was a very old man. I think, although perhaps I am taking a liberty, that the Lord could not really reveal the essential matter to Moses in his earlier more vigorous and active type of manhood. You see, Moses was a man of 120 years old and he had a history of deep experience with the Lord. He had a lot of observation. Wisdom comes from observation as well as experience. Some people have a lot of experience, but not a lot of wisdom because they do not observe things. Wisdom comes from experience and observation, reflection and meditation. We see by observation what is happening. We observe in another light what the Lord is doing, how He is reacting.

Moses was a man of great observation. He watched and he watched and he observed and he observed. I believe that when he was first called to give the law, it must have broken Moses' heart to see the reaction of the people. Then there was that long history of rebellion, and murmuring, of gainsaying, and contradiction. Everything he said they sort of said, "Oh, Moses!" They did not have time for Moses or his ministry and do you know the amazing thing, the most vital thing? When he saw not just one, but multitudes destroyed because of their rebellion and murmuring, so that in the end that whole generation was wiped out, including his brother and his sister, and he alone was left with Joshua and Caleb, don't you think that out of that kind of agonising experience and observation he learned about the people? What did he learn? He learnt that the basic, elementary necessity is love and that, without love, you can only drag a people through the wilderness and even then, they would choose to die in the wilderness. It was love that was needed to, somehow or other, fire up those people and give them faith. Faith worketh by love to please God and go over into the unknown and take the land.

Do you see what I mean? It was simply that, in a most wonderful way, Moses, at the end, came right through to the root of his own problem. Why, why, why with all his revelation of God, with his mighty ministry, with this tremendous breaking in of God so that he actually saw Him, this cloud of fire by night, this pillar of cloud by day ... Why, why, why? People often say nowadays, "If only we could see." People often say, "We have had a weekly provision of ministry, have we not?" Yet, you still have people who go back. You still have people who contradict. You still have people who murmur. You still have people in rebellion! Seeing the Lord, even if the Lord came here and stood here visibly in the midst, would not affect the situation. Within a week you could have a terrific eruption, and half the company would be up in arms— that's it. Just the week before they were trusting in the Lord. May we see that this is not what you see; it is not what you know. It is the heart of love for the Lord. You have here a great secret. The heart is the focal point of everything, and the love of the heart is the focal point of everything.

So, Moses, at the end of his life, has come right to the root of the problem. He has the explanation for a generation dying.

He has the explanation for a generation that saw so much and yet, somehow, contradicts it and fought with the Lord. Deuteronomy is the ministry, I think, of a man with a broken heart. That is why I believe that again and again, in this book of Deuteronomy, you find Moses subtly saying, "The Lord is not going to let me go." Have you noticed that? Not once, but again and again, Moses brings it to a personal level, "and the Lord won't let me go." He also has learned a big lesson in the wilderness.

Note too, how "the Lord" is brought into the book of Deuteronomy in such a way that everything is related to Him; it is always "the Lord." In fact, without being irreverent, you almost find that to read "Jehovah," for instance in the Standard Version, is almost tiring after a while because Jehovah comes in so much—Jehovah this, Jehovah that, Jehovah the other. This is in relation to Jehovah, that in relation to Jehovah, the other in relation to Jehovah. What is it really? Why does Moses use the name of the Lord everywhere? Because, I believe again, it is linked to this testimony of love. It is simply that the Lord is presenting Himself. Not against them. Not so much for salvation. He is presenting Himself as a Person to be loved, to be taken, to be possessed. He is asking you to return that love. This then is the heart of the book of Deuteronomy.

Outline of the Book

I am not going to spend so long upon the outline of the book. The most important thing with this type of book, with its method and style, is what I said about the key to the book. I think that really has covered it. You can read the book now with that in mind. Now we will follow up with a few more facts that I think will help us.

A New Generation

What is the outline of this book of Deuteronomy? There are three things that I should like you to note. First of all, Moses is addressing a new generation. The old generation has died, hence the need for this review. He is speaking to a generation, many of whom had actually seen the things spoken about, but they were very young, only up to the age of 20. They had now come to the point where their parents have died, all their relatives have died (except their younger cousins and cousins their own age) and now they were listening to Moses reinterpret and review the parchments.

The Land and the Lord's Purpose

The second thing I want you to notice is the emphasis in the book of Deuteronomy upon the land. You will notice that the emphasis is upon God's purpose, the land, and the possession of it. I think a few scriptures would help us in this matter.

> "But Jehovah hath taken you, and brought you forth out
> of the iron furnace, out of Egypt, to be unto him a people
> of inheritance, as at this day. Furthermore Jehovah
> was angry with me for your sakes, and sware that I
> should not go over the Jordan, and that I should not go
> in unto that good land, which Jehovah thy God giveth

thee for an inheritance." (Deuteronomy 4:20–21)

The Lord continually stresses out of what He has taken them, and into what He is taking them. All the way through the book of Deuteronomy, He is stressing out of what He has taken them and into what He is going to take them.

> *"And because he loved thy fathers, therefore he chose*
> *their seed after them, and brought thee out with his*
> *presence, with his great power, out of Egypt; to drive*
> *out nations from before thee greater and mightier than*
> *thou, to bring thee in, to give thee their land for an*
> *inheritance, as at this day." (Deuteronomy 4:37–38)*

Did you notice the play on words? "He brought thee out ... to bring thee in." "He brought thee out ... to bring thee in."

> *"and he brought us out from thence, that he might*
> *bring us in, to give us the land which he sware*
> *unto our fathers." (Deuteronomy 6:23)*

Here are just three references to something. If you want to run a line, you would find that nearly every chapter has some reference to out of what they were brought and into what they were being brought. So there is really a great emphasis in this book upon the purpose of God and the land.

Now, what can we learn from that? What is the promised land always a symbol of in Scripture? It is not a symbol of the church, is it? It is a symbol of our inheritance, yes, but what is our inheritance really? It is Christ Himself, the fulness of Christ. The promised land is always a symbol in Scripture of the fulness of God, the riches to be explored, the treasure to be found, the land to farm, yielding increase in its abundance. It speaks of the fulness of Christ, a land flowing with milk and honey. Everything is abundant and full about this land. There is also something permanent about this land.

The Fulness of God

Now, you see, Deuteronomy is speaking to us about the fulness of God. Now, for one moment take your mind right back to our earlier studies. Genesis spoke of God's purpose—His beginning—how He dealt with individuals with a tremendous purpose in mind. Exodus spoke of the redemption of a people and the revelation of His dwelling place. God was going to build a dwelling place out of redeemed ones. They were the stones quarried. Now He was going to build the living stones together. Leviticus spoke to us of how we could become part of God's dwelling place when we are such sinful, poor material. Numbers spoke about the absolute necessity of our being responsible if we were going to come into our full inheritance. Deuteronomy tells us that the fulness of God is God's great object. Even the church is a means to an end, we must remember. The church is "the fulness of Him that filleth all in all," it says in Ephesians 1:23. "... His body, the fulness of Him that filleth all in all."

The fulness of God then is linked to the church, but the church is a means to an end. This simply means that no one can experience, or come to, or achieve, or attain to the fulness of God without knowing a deep experience of the church. The church is the means to the end. This is why the book of Revelation was written. It was written to show to us that here, in our locality, as we are built into what God is doing here on earth with all its difficulties and contradictions and so much else, so many problems, God is building us into something eternal, which is to be the vessel of His fulness for all eternity, something which is not in itself the end, but the beginning.

I do not believe that the last chapters of the Bible are the end (like so many people foolishly believe), that it is the curtain. It is the curtain as far as revelations go, but it is only actually the curtain on time. It is the beginning of eternity. I believe that we have a tremendous future that none of us know about, none of us would even be able to dream about that is before us in the future.

What is God's fulness? Scientists have tried to unravel something of the fulness of this universe. They have spent centuries on some things and still have only touched the very circumference of it. They have hardly got anywhere with it.

What about the fulness of God? Do you think the Bible holds all the fulness of God? I don't. I believe it has enough for us and all that is necessary for life down here and our ways during it, but the fulness of God is inexhaustible. That is something that if you and I are so keen to be a part of what God is doing here on this earth, then we are going to be part of that in eternity. We shall be the vessels in eternity. We shall be exploring the fulness of God! What a thing! What a wonderful, mighty thing to be able to be launched upon such an endless exploration.

So, Deuteronomy ends the Pentateuch. In some ways, it is the end of the Word. In one way, it is the end of one part of the Word.

The Pentateuch is quite watertight in many ways, and, in that sense, tells us: here you come to the fulness of God.

A Specific Place in the Land

The other thing that I want you to note because it is bound up with this is that there is a specific place in the land which is continually referred to. Let us look at this because it needs a little bit of investigation. From chapter 12 onward, a particular place in the land is continually referred to as the only place acceptable to God. Well, that is strange. That is very strange. Isn't anywhere in the fulness of Christ acceptable? Why does God say that there is a certain place in the land alone which is acceptable to Him? Don't go offering your offerings anywhere; there is only one place in the whole land where He will accept them. If you offer them elsewhere they won't be accepted.

> "But unto the place which Jehovah your God shall
> choose out of all your tribes, to put his name
> there, even unto his habitation shall ye seek, and
> thither thou shalt come ..." (Deuteronomy 12:5)

> "Then it shall come to pass that to the place which Jehovah
> your God shall choose, to cause his name to dwell there,
> thither shall ye bring all that I command you: your
> burnt-offerings, and your sacrifices, your tithes, and the
> heave-offering of your hand, and all your choice vows
> which ye vow unto Jehovah." (Deuteronomy 12:11)

Verses 13, 14: "Take heed to thyself that thou offer not thy
burnt-offerings in every place that thou seest; but in the
place which Jehovah shall choose in one of thy tribes, there
thou shalt offer thy burnt-offerings, and there thou shalt
do all that I command thee." (Deuteronomy 12:13–14)

We cannot read all the references to this place where the Lord
has caused His name to dwell, but from chapter 12 onward it
continually comes in in all kinds of aspects.

"but at the place which Jehovah thy God shall choose, to
cause his name to dwell in, there thou shalt sacrifice the
Passover at even, at the going down of the sun, at the season
that thou camest forth out of Egypt." (Deuteronomy 16:6)

This is the Passover. Up to now everyone has eaten it in their
homes. Now they are told, "You are not allowed to sacrifice the
Passover lamb in your home. You must sacrifice in the place,
which the Lord thy God shall choose".

Then in the feast that we know as Pentecost:

"and thou shalt rejoice before Jehovah thy God, thou, and thy son,
and thy daughter ... in the place which Jehovah thy God shall
choose, to cause his name to dwell there." (Deuteronomy 16:11)

Then the Feast of Tabernacles:

"Three times in a year shall all thy males appear
before [the Lord] thy God in the place which he

shall choose ..." (Deuteronomy 16:16a)

We find that this place is mentioned in the land.

"When all Israel is come to appear before [the Lord] thy God in the place which he shall choose, thou shalt read this law before all Israel in their hearing." (Deuteronomy 31:11)

This is the reading of the law which Moses enjoined. So it is not only the land which is God's object, but evidently, this place in the land is the only place which is acceptable to God. There is only one place, in other words, in the whole land, the circumference of the land, where you can take your sacrifice and make your vow. What does this speak to us about? What does this show to us? It illustrates to us simply what I have been saying about the fulness of God: we cannot come to the fulness of God except by way of the house of God. The house of God is the only way that we can come to the fulness of God. We can be Christ's, we can know something of all that Christ is, yet not be accepted with God. We have not tasted a full salvation; we are living a partial type of salvation. We are in and yet we are not really accepted. Our service, our ministry, our offerings, our attitude, is not really acceptable because it is not related to the place. It does not matter where you live in the whole land. If you are related to God's house in a right way, you are accepted.

Later on, Solomon takes up this very thought. It does not matter where you are, so long as you turn toward the house, lift up your hands toward it, and pray to the God of Jerusalem. God will hear and will answer. He said, it does not matter if you are dispersed to the far ends of the earth, if you will only turn toward the house of God at Jerusalem, lift up your hands and pray, God will hear, will answer, and will deliver you. This is just an illustration to us, the relatedness to the house of God. The fulness of Christ is related to the house of God.

We find that there is a four-fold division in the book of Deuteronomy. Firstly, their history is reviewed from chapter one to chapter four. Then the law is reinterpreted to them from chapter 4–26. The covenant is reviewed with them from chapter 27–30 and then we have the farewell of Moses. We need not spend very long upon this, but do let us look a little more at these four divisions.

History Reviewed

In the first division, Deuteronomy 1–4, Moses reviews the history of the people and he draws out five simple things. The first is the sovereignty of the Lord in their history. If the Lord is ever going to bring us into the fulness of Christ it is going to be sovereignly. While there must be reaction in us and a response in us, it is going to be the sovereignty of God that gets us through. This is through the Lord's sovereignty. He loves you. He gained you. He led. All the way through, Moses is stressing the fact that it is Jehovah that does it. Jehovah gains us. Jehovah is leading. Jehovah stirs us up. Jehovah is fighting the battle. All this is the sovereignty of the Lord.

The second thing we learn about the history that he brings out is the Lord's lordship over His people: He must be Lord. Over their life, over their homes, over their positions, over their careers, over their work, over their movement, the Lord must be Lord. That is why He takes them back to the book of Numbers and elsewhere in their history and he just lets them know that it is the heart of God and the presence of the Lord which is the basic thing about their going on with Him. Are we related to His Lordship? Is He really Lord? No tribe must be out of place. No tent in any tribe must be out of place. The Levites must not be out of place. Everyone was in position for the conflict. Everyone was given something to do. They had to come under the Lordship of the Lord.

Then another thing Moses speaks about, which he learned from their history, is this: faith in the Lord is absolutely necessary. He does dwell upon the spies going in. "When the Lord told you to go over, you would not go, and we spent 40 years in the desert." Faith. Faith is over against natural wisdom and reason. Logic. Logic is a terrible thing. Rationalism is a terrible thing if the Lord does not break it. Once it is broken, it can be used of God, but when it is unbroken, in all its rigidity and its unbelief, it cannot be used. Here you have it: faith is absolutely necessary if the Lord is going to get His people through with the fulness of God. You will never get there otherwise. Logic will tell us that we cannot get there. There is too much against us and too much within us to stop us. We will never get there.

Then again, he brings out another thing, which I think is very wonderful. He tells them what he had learnt from reviewing the history of his people. He has learnt that the Lord is the meaning of their life. He said, "He is thy life and the length of thy days."

He is thy life. What does it mean? It just means this: that the Lord delivers. The Lord instructs. The Lord interprets. The Lord fights the battle. The Lord defeats the enemies. It is the Lord all the way through. If you take the Lord away, you are left with nothing. Put the Lord in and you have everything. This is just the history of the people of God. Take the Lord away and what have you got? The Jews are left with nothing. What are they left with? Commercialism. That is about the only thing we have ever gotten from the Jews, and the Lord said it here in the book of Deuteronomy: "You will lend to all nations." Nations will always be in her debt because of the book of Deuteronomy. That, the Lord gave her.

What have the Jews left us? They have left us no great monuments to their civilisation like the pyramids or anything else. They have left us no great cities as such. We have no wonderful record of such. We have the Bible and we know that alone has come in a most remarkable and sovereign way. The Jews were a poor people. You see, the Lord was the means. Take the Lord away from a Jew and he is nothing. Put the Lord into the Jew and he is great. The Lord is the glory of Israel; Israel's glory is the Lord.

The last thing we learned in this review of history is that their key to the history is the love of the Lord. As we have read already, "because He loveth you, He chose you." It says in Deuteronomy 4:37, "And because He loved thy fathers, therefore He chose their seed after them." The key to their history was the love of God. Moses speaks of three things: he speaks of God's faithfulness, of God's mercy, and of God's jealousy. These three things are bound up in love. If God loves us, He is faithful to us. If God loves us—He is merciful to us. If God loves us, He is jealous for us. It is a terrible thing to meet the jealousy of God. A terrible thing. If you are loved by God, God is very jealous for you. That is why the Lord will sometimes put us through some hard ways, just because He loves us—not the wrong kind of ways, the right kind. Moses in his review of history reveals to us that it is love. Why did the Lord deal so harshly? Why did the Lord slay them? Why did the Lord turn against them? Because the Lord was so jealous to have a people for Himself.

The Law Reinterpreted

Then you see the law reinterpreted, and I can only leave this with you from chapters 4–26, love is the key to the law. If you want to find that out, you will find that again and again in these few chapters. In Deuteronomy 5:10, we have exactly what we find in Exodus 20:6. Then if you go to Deuteronomy 6:5 you find, "and thou shalt love Jehovah thy God with all thy heart, and with all thy soul, and with all thy might." In chapter 7, verse 9 it says, "Know therefore that Jehovah thy God, He is God, the faithful God, who keepeth covenant and lovingkindness with them that love Him." Then, look at verse 13, "He will love thee, and bless thee," and in chapter 10 verses 12 and 15, "And now, Israel, what doth Jehovah thy God require of thee, but to fear Jehovah thy God, to walk in all His ways, and to love Him ... Only Jehovah had a delight in thy fathers to love them, and He chose their seed after them."

This is reiterated again and again, right the way through. Love is the key to the law. The ten commandments were given because the Lord wants a people who could love Him. Love was behind the law. Love is the answer to giving the Lord His rights. If we love the Lord, we will give the Lord His rights.

What are the Lord's rights? You will find them from chapter 12 on. What is the Lord's right? The place which He shall choose. That is the Lord's right. It is not where you pick to make your offering, where you choose, where your eyes see, where somehow you feel you agree, where you feel it would be nice to go. But the place which the Lord thy God should choose to cause His name to dwell, there thou shall offer a lamb. That is the right of the Lord.

If you go on you find that the Lord is proving people in a rather mysterious way. He allows some false prophets to come amongst them. In Deuteronomy 13:1, "If there arise in the midst of thee a prophet, or a dreamer of dreams ..." Why does the Lord allow false prophets to arise in the midst of His people and say things that turn everyone upside down. They say they have a revelation. They say the Lord has broken in and told them something. They are big. They are mighty. They have something tremendous. These people are raised up because there is ground for the enemy. They come forward with their great ideas and so on. Why does the Lord not stamp them out? Because it says in Deuteronomy 13:3, "... for the Lord your God proveth you, to know whether ye love Jehovah your God with all your heart and with all your soul."

If you love the Lord with all your heart and with all your soul, you are given a kind of discrimination. You are given a discernment. People have a stupid idea that love is sentimental, non-discriminatory. It is nothing of the kind. Love is the most discriminating thing in the universe. You cannot love everything. It is discriminating. By the fall, we have a wrong kind of discrimination, but in the Lord we have a right kind of discrimination. We are not sentimental; we do not shut our eyes. We see, and when there are false prophets and dreamers of dreams, we see. We do not walk in their ways, and we do not hearken to their counsel. We just close our ears and we withdraw. Thus you see, love is the answer for giving the Lord His rights.

Dear Reader,

Unfortunately, the audio of this ministry was cut short. However, Lance did a thorough outline and study guide to accompany this message, which is included in the next section of this book. Please note that the information for the remainder of the message begins in the outline: The Law Reinterpreted, under heading 11 b. We hope you find this helpful to continue in your study of Deuteronomy.

The Editor

14.
Deuteronomy
Study Guide

Introduction

The name "Deuteronomy" is taken from the Greek, and means "the second law," or "the repetition of the law." The Hebrew title is taken from the first sentence of the book and means, "these are the words." The beauty of Deuteronomy is hardly anywhere excelled, nor its direct simplicity of language.

In many ways, this book of the Pentateuch is different from the other four books. It is what the Gospel of John is to the other gospels, a spiritual interpretation and underlining of what has gone before.

Deuteronomy is prophetic. It is not mere teaching and regulations, but it is the setting forth of the heart of the matter, the inner principle of the law. It is not the mere repetition of the law for a new generation, but an interpretation of its true meaning. It goes beyond even that, for it is the interpretation of their past, present and future, their calling and destiny as the people of God.

We should note that, apart from the Psalms, it is the most quoted book in the New Testament (quoted or alluded to 96 times approximately). In the Old Testament it is quoted approximately 356 times, and is closely bound up with Leviticus (61 times), and Numbers (74 times). The Lord Jesus, in the temptation, used Deuteronomy three times when He answered Satan.

With Deuteronomy, the five books of the Hebrew *Torah* (Law) are completed. The foundation upon which the whole Old Testament was to be built was finished with this book.

Authorship and Date

There has been much controversy as to the authorship and date of Deuteronomy, but it is manifestly the work of Moses, if not exactly as we now have it, basically his work. See Deuteronomy 31:24. Some believe that later scribes edited Deuteronomy and that the form in which we now have it dates from Ezra's day.

Others believe that it is a "pious fraud" written either in the time of King Josiah and was the book of the law "found" in the temple (See II Kings 22:8) or was written in the post exilic period. It is hard to believe that our Lord Jesus answered the Devil three times by quoting from a "pious fraud", without Satan raising the point! Furthermore, both Peter and Stephen refer to Moses as the author of Deuteronomy. See Acts 3:22–23; Acts 7:37. It seems therefore, reasonably clear that Moses was the author of this book and also as reasonably clear that there are a few additions, particularly the account of Moses' death. This was probably written by either Joshua or one of the Levites.

The eight discourses were, obviously, first given orally, see chapter 1, verse 3, and then written in book form in Deuteronomy 31:9, 24. It was written in the uplands of Moab, overlooking the promised land in the month before Moses died, approximately 1400 BC when he was 120 years of age. He must have known that Israel was soon to pass over Jordan, and that he, therefore, had little time available. Deuteronomy is the work of a man deeply wrought upon by God.

The book covers the 40 years between the exodus from Egypt and the crossing of the Jordan, and is given in retrospect. It would have taken Moses about 5 weeks to rehearse. See Deuteronomy 1:3. "In the 40th year, the 11th month, the 1st day. Joshua 4:19. "In the 41st year, the 1st month, the 10th day, Israel crossed the Jordan".

Key to the Book

In spite of its Greek name "Repetition of the Law", the key to Deuteronomy is not the Word of God, nor the Law, but the essential element and quality that He is forever seeking, and which alone can truly answer Him—love. This has hardly been mentioned in the Bible up to this point, although implied and illustrated. The one exception is Exodus 20:6

Everywhere we find now that the basic and necessary quality which God looks for in His own, is love. (See Deuteronomy 5:10; 6:5; 7:9; 10:12, 18, 19; 11:1, 13, 22; 13:3; 19:9; 30:6, 16, 20.) We discover, moreover, that behind all God's ways and dealings with His own is in His love. (See Deuteronomy 4:37; 7:6–13; 10:15; 23:5; 33:3.) From all this, it is clear that the only thing that can satisfy God is love, and that divine love alone can keep us in the will and the ways of God. We ought to note that with the word "love", a number of other words are associated:

"Obey", "cleave", see e.g. Deuteronomy 10:20 cp v.18, 19 "Fear", "serve", "keep".

Note e.g. Deuteronomy 10:20 cp. Deuteronomy 10:12, 19; 11:1, 22; 13:4; 30:20

Moses was now an old man with a long history of experience and observation. He had seen not only the acts of God, but supremely, he had understood the ways of God. His life had been an instruction in God's ways. Now at the end of his life, by the grace of God, and through the Holy Spirit, he puts his finger on the vital constituent without which all is meaningless. He rehearses their history in the light of divine love. He repeats the Law with this new emphasis and depth.

Notice also how the name of the Lord is mentioned in relation to everything and everyone in this book. His name is continually reiterated. This too is linked with love. (See Deuteronomy 5:11; 6:13; 10:20; 12:5, 11, 21; 14:23, 24; 16:6, 11; 18:5, 7, 19, 20, 22; 26:2; 28:58; 32:3)

Outline of the Book

We need to bear three things in mind:

1. There was, with the exception of two men, a completely new generation. Hence the need of the review.

2. The emphasis upon the land and the Lord's purpose. This is the context of the book. (See Deuteronomy 4:20, 21, 37, 38; 6:23.)

3. A specific place in the land is referred to continually, from chapter 12 onwards, as the only place acceptable to God. (See Deuteronomy12:5, 11, 13, 14; 16:6, 11,16; 31:11_

I. History Reviewed

(Deuteronomy 1:1–4:43)

A. The sovereignty of the Lord over Israel's whole history

B. The Lord's lordship over His people—their life, their home, their work, their movements etc.

C. The absolute necessity of faith in the Lord—the need to trust the Lord and His ability.

D. The Lord is the meaning of their life—He delivers them, He defeats their enemies, He provides for them, He guides, He interprets, He instructs.

E. The key to their history is the love of God—His faithfulness, His mercy, and His jealousy over them.

II. The Law Reinterpreted

(Deuteronomy 4:44–26:19)

A. Love is the key—not only to the giving of the law, but also to the keeping of it. See chapters 5:10; 6:5–7; 7:9, 13; 10:12, 15; 11:1, 13, 22.

B. Love is the answer to giving the Lord His rights (See Deuteronomy 13:3, 4; 15:12–18). (A picture of true service)

C. We ought to note that underlying all the many laws to do with our relations to one another is this matter of love. Love for God must be expressed in love for our brother and even the stranger in our midst. Divine love is the strength of the corporate life.

D. Note:

1. The repetition of the ten commandments (Deuteronomy 5) Their value summed up and the heart of the matter emphasised.

2. The privileges and the perils of election (Deuteronomy 6–11) To be the elect people of God has both its glorious privileges and its very grave responsibilities. Love alone can keep us in the ways of God.

3. The dwelling place of God (Deuteronomy 12–16) The desire of God to dwell amongst His people is born of His love for us. Mark the place of worship— the one sanctuary which He has chosen (the oneness of Christ) and the purity of worship—holiness.

4. The love of God expressed in the execution of justice and the administration of government (Deuteronomy 16:18–26). All these many laws embody and express the love of God. We do not often associate justice and government with divine love, but true justice and government are for our good. Behind the whole concept of such justice and government is the love of God.

III. The Covenant Renewed

(Deuteronomy 27–30)

A. The stones containing the Law were to be set up on Mt. Ebal. We then have the solemn warning as to blessing and curse (Deuteronomy 27–28)

B. To go on with the Lord means blessing, increase, instruction etc.

C. To go back from the Lord is to lose all the meaning of one's life.

D. The renewal of the covenant (Deuteronomy29–30)

E. Note carefully Deuteronomy 30:15–20

IV. The Farewell of Moses

A. The song of Moses (Deuteronomy 31–32)

B. The blessing of Moses (Deuteronomy 33)

C. The death of Moses (Deuteronomy 34)

Message of the Book

This is the summing up of the Pentateuch, and the setting forth of that one basic element which will give rise to everything else. That basic element is love. Without that kind of love all our worship, living, and service becomes a caricature of the real thing. God can never be satisfied without this love, even if everything else is in order. It is the essential element, which alone can answer Him. 1 Corinthians 13 is the best summary of Deuteronomy; it encapsulates the purpose of God and the service of God. Cold, formal obedience, a mere technical knowledge and exactness, cannot ever satisfy the heart of God, nor reach His end.

Recommended books

Notes on Deuteronomy
    C.H. Mackintosh

Questions

1. What is the main message of the book of Deuteronomy? (Write a few sentences)

Why do you think this is so important? Give references, if you can, to support your reasons.

2. Can you find the outstanding prophecy in Deuteronomy concerning Christ?

3. Why is the book of Deuteronomy so important in the Bible?

4. Read chapter 20:1–20. What lessons could Christians find there about spiritual warfare?

5. Read chapter 7 and 9:1–15. State in a sentence why God requires the destruction of the Canaanite nations. Can you draw any lessons from this, for the Christian life?

6. Read 7:6–10; 9:6–29. Do you find anything there that tells you of God's attitude to His people?

Do you find anything surprising in His attitude?

7. Read 7:21–8:10. What can you find out about spiritual growth in this passage?

8. Read 31:14–32:53. Write a paragraph on the faithfulness of God to His own purposes.

9. Chapters 29 and 30 tell us something about covenant relationship and responsibilities. Say something about the work of Christ for us, as prefigured in:
a) Deuteronomy 29: 12–15 (the gospel for the Gentiles)

b) Deuteronomy30: 5–6 (Colossians 2:1–11)

c) Deuteronomy 30:19

10. Read chapter 4:31–43, and 19:1–21. Does this speak to you, in any way, about the work of Christ, on behalf of sinners?

11. In Deuteronomy, we find that Moses makes the following speeches listed below. Give a title to each of these speeches, and write one or two sentences giving some idea of what Moses is saying.

Example: 1:5–4:40
The History of God's People Reviewed.

In this speech, Moses reminds Israel of the way in which God has led them, reminding them of His sovereignty, as well as His love, patience and faithfulness to His promises, in spite of their unfaithfulness to Him. Moses impressed upon the people that such a God is utterly to be trusted and that obedience to Him will mean great blessing for them.

a. Deuteronomy 1:5–4:40

b. Deuteronomy 4:44–26:19

c. Deuteronomy 27:1–28:68

d. Deuteronomy 29:1–30:20

e. Deuteronomy 31:1–23

f. Deuteronomy 31:24–29

g. Deuteronomy 32:1–47

h. Deuteronomy 33:1–29

12. Examine the following verses. Deuteronomy 12:5, 11–13, 17–18, 21; 14:23–25; 15:20; 16:2, 6, 7, 11, 15, 16; 17:8; 18:6, 7; 26:2; 31:11. Where was this place that the Lord was going to choose?

What is the significance of this for Christians today? Give scripture references in your answer.

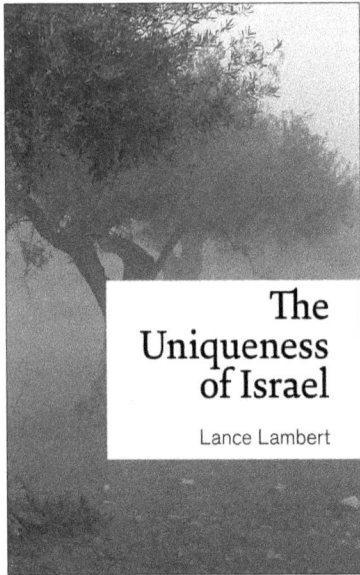

The Uniqueness of Israel

Woven into the fabric of Jewish existence there is an undeniable uniqueness. There is bitter controversy over the subject of Israel, but time itself will establish the truth about this nation's place in God's plan. For Lance Lambert, the Lord Jesus is the key that unlocks Jewish history He is the key not only to their fall, but also to their restoration. For in spite of the fact that they rejected Him, He has not rejected them.

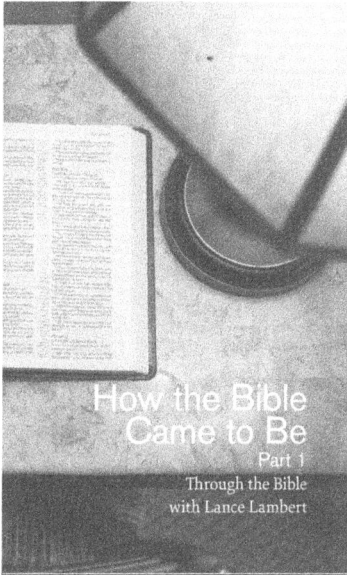

How the Bible Came to Be: Part 1

How is the Bible still as applicable in the 21st century as it was when it was first penned? How did so many authors, with different backgrounds and over thousands of years, write something so perfectly fitting with one another?

Lance Lambert breaks down these, and many other questions in this first volume of his series teaching through the Bible. He lays a firm foundation for going on to study the Word of the living God.

And ye shall seek me, and find me, when ye shall search for me
with all your heart.
Jeremiah 29:13

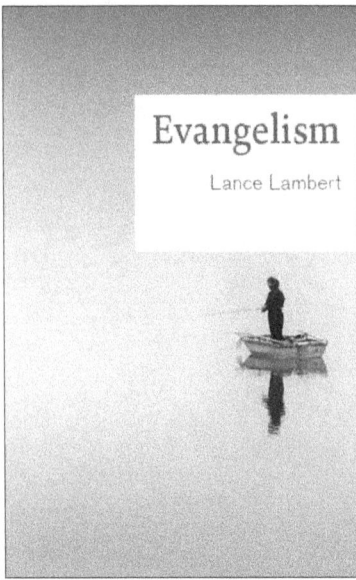

Evangelism

What is God's purpose in evangelism?

It is clear that the Word of God commands us to preach the gospel to every creature, to go into the whole world and make disciples of all nations baptising them in the name of the Father, the Son and the Holy Spirit.

So how do we do it?

In "Evangelism" Lance opens the scriptures to reveal how the church can practically and effectively preach the gospel to the unsaved world, by revealing to them in scripture their need for a Saviour, the work of the Saviour, and how to receive the Saviour. He explains practical means of winning souls and how to follow-up with the newly saved to make disciples of the Lord Jesus. Evangelism is the way by which we gather the materials for the house of God.

So faith comes by hearing, and hearing through the word of Christ.

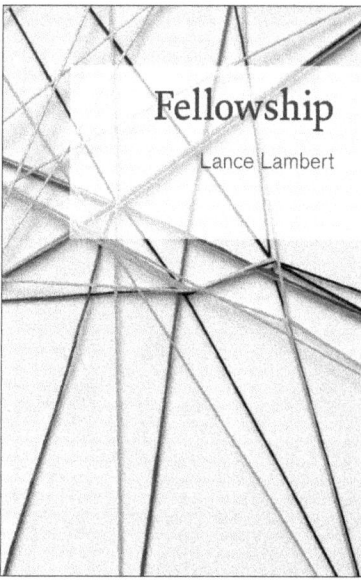

Fellowship

Ephesians 2 says that we in the household of God are to be built up together for a habitation for God in the Spirit.

What does this mean for you and me to be built up together with other believers? How should we contribute to the building work of Christ? What are the principles that govern this fellowship and building work?

In this current volume, Lance Lambert addresses these and other questions. He shares how "God has always desired a dwelling place in which He can express Himself, reveal Himself and manifest Himself, as it were, a place in which He can find His home."

Thank the Lord this is His heart's desire–to be with us and let us know Him. How blessed we are!